ENDORSEMENTS FOR

CRUCIFORM IDENTITY

This book is a delicious reflection upon the truths of Romans 8, a tonic for the soul. Written by a pastor-theologian, this application of the gospel will both inform your mind and delight your heart.

—**Dr. Andrew Hebert**, Lead Pastor of *Paramount Baptist Church, Amarillo, Texas.*

***

Theologically robust, devotionally strong and practically rich, this book is a great primer into the unexplored beauty of the believer's union with Christ. Michael has helped us make the mystery of our union with Christ a more concrete and sanctifying truth. Very thankful for this life giving and grace filled little book!

—**Clint Pressley**, Senior Pastor of *Hickory Grove Baptist Church, Charlotte, North Carolina.*

***

I'm sure you've struggled with your identity and self-worth. We all have. Where did you turn in those moments? Where will you point others in their crises of identity? I recommend Michael Cooper's Cruciform Identity as a helpful starting point. In it, Cooper rightly argues that "the cure for our identity crisis is to find our identity in Christ." Grounding his counsel in Romans 8, Cooper explains the importance of an oft-neglected doctrine – union with Christ. Read this book and let the author guide you through a study of Romans 8. Once you grasp the reality that you are in Christ and Christ is in you, you will respond in joy-filled praise and faith-filled assurance. For God, in Christ, is the one who establishes your identity and your self-worth.

— **Juan R. Sanchez**, Senior Pastor, *High Pointe Baptist Church, Austin, Texas,* author of *The Leadership Formula: Develop the Next Generation of Leaders in the Church.*

***

One of the biggest crisis that people suffer with today is an identity crisis. Everyone has the same great need – an identity change. And, only Jesus can make that happen. That is why my friend, Michael Cooper's book, is so very important. He shows how our union with Christ changes our identity! Make sure you buy a copy for yourself and one for someone else that needs it. It is a must read.

—**Shane Pruitt**, National Next Gen Director, *North American Mission Board (NAMB).* Author, *9 Common Lies Christians Believe.*

***

As Christians, we are crucified with Christ and yet we live. It is in this identity that we find purpose, power, and life in abundance. Michael takes a deep dive into our identity as living image bearers of Christ Jesus. This work is not only deeply doctrinal but also immediately practical. I challenge you to read these pages slowly and carefully. Consider how, as a believer in Jesus, your identity is completely wrapped up in your relationship with the incarnated, crucified, resurrected, and exalted Christ. And choose to embrace the joy and freedom that are found in the cruciform identity of your new birth in Him.

—Dr. Tony Wolfe, Director of Pastor and Church Relations for the *Southern Baptists of Texas Convention*.

***

Here is a captivating devotional feast by a young scholar and passionate pastor who could not be dull if he tried, as has often been said of William Barclay, the eminent Scottish New Testament scholar. It is clear that Michael has worked with the text of the Greek, knows the structural, theological, hermeneutical issues of the paragraph, is conversant with contemporary scholarship, but is unimpressed with his own scholarly erudition and hence efficiently pursues his goal of being a theological intermediary of profound biblical truth. Take. Read. Be blessed.

—Dr. H. Leroy Metts, Distinguished Senior Professor of *Greek and New Testament, Criswell College in Dallas, Texas*.

***

Michael Cooper is one of the most biblically and theologically faithful pastors I know, and this little book is proof. Cruciform Identity is easy-to-read and yet packed with deep truth. Pastors: get this into the hands of your people!

—Brandon D. Smith, Assistant Professor of *Theology and New Testament at Cedarville University*, author of *Rooted and They Spoke of Me*.

Michael Cooper

***

Michael Cooper's short but potent work on our spiritual identity in Christ is one of the best books I've read on this subject. He writes with one eye on Scripture and the other on personal experience. The combination is effective. Who we are in Christ and knowing who we are in Christ is the key to living the successful Christian life! This book will tell you the what, the how, and the why. Highly recommended!

—David Allen, Distinguished Professor of *Preaching at Southwestern Baptist Theological Seminary*.

CRUCIFORM IDENTITY

Union with Christ and Christian Formation

MICHAEL COOPER

Published by KHARIS PUBLISHING, imprint of KHARIS MEDIA LLC.

Copyright © 2020 Michael Cooper

ISBN-13: 978-1-946277-79-4

ISBN-10: 1-946277-79-7

Library of Congress Control Number: 2020943762

All rights reserved. This book or parts thereof may not be reproduced in any form, stored in a retrieval system, or transmitted in any form by any means - electronic, mechanical, photocopy, recording, or otherwise - without prior written permission of the publisher, except as provided by United States of America copyright law.

Scripture quotations marked CSB have been taken from the Christian Standard Bible®, Copyright © 2017 by Holman Bible Publishers. Used by permission. Christian Standard Bible® and CSB® are federally registered trademarks of Holman Bible Publishers

All KHARIS PUBLISHING products are available at special quantity discounts for bulk purchase for sales promotions, premiums, fund-raising, and educational needs. For details, contact:

Kharis Media LLC
Tel: 1-479-599-8657
support@kharispublishing.com
www.kharispublishing.com

Kailie Alexa
Sophia Grace
Lydia Joy

You are my earthly joys who direct my affections to our Heavenly Father.

ACKNOWLEDGMENTS

I want to thank the members of Grace Community Church in Mabank, Texas. They have provided me the opportunity to preach and teach God's Word. This book is the byproduct of our ministry together. They have shaped me as a pastor and I am humbled to serve as their under-shepherd. I pray that the material of this book and my ministry at GCC reflects Paul's own words, "Death works in us, but life in you." I thank my GCC staff: Cindy Owens (director of ministries) and Nick Corrado (associate pastor) who heard about this book before it was in print. You helped me flesh out ideas and concepts as they swirled in my mind! A special thanks to Stacy Ross, LaRue Monsivais, Pam Wilkerson, Bruce Martin and others who offered various insights along the way. I am grateful for other friends who helped in the writing process: Brandon Smith, Matt Henslee, Paul Garcia, Tony Wolfe, and Andrew Hebert.

I am indebted to many mentors who have encouraged me in this cruciform journey. I owe much to Jason Points who introduced me to the concept of *cruciformity* during my fourth semester of college. Many of the thoughts contained in this book reflect our theological conversations that stem from over a decade of friendship. This book would have not been possible without the encouragement of Dr. Roy Metts, New Testament and Greek Professor at Criswell College.

He taught me the exegetical nuances of the Greek text and the rich truths concerning New Testament Theology. But more than anything, he taught me to love Jesus through the rigorous study of the Bible. I have sought to make "my work, my worship to Christ."

Most importantly, I could not have written this book without the love of my wife and our girls. Kailie is the visible demonstration of cruciform love and humility. Her gracious words and tender care motivate me to serve Jesus more faithfully. The precious encouragement that flows from the lips of Sophia and Lydia motivates me to pursue the throne of grace. The Lord has been kind by providing me with these three who, by the Spirit, aid in my cruciformity.

CONTENTS

	Preface	xiii
	Introduction	xv
1	Identity Crisis	1
2	Cruciform Identity and the Cross	13
3	Cruciform Identity and the Sprit	27
4	Cruciform Identity and the Resurrection	37
5	Cruciform Identity and the Sovereignty of God	49
6	Cruciform Identity and Eternal Security	61
7	The Truth of Our Cruciform Identity	69
8	Experiencing Our Cruciform Identity	83
9	Identity Crisis Averted	95

PREFACE

This book was birthed out of personal experience and a desire to understand the truth of my own identity in Christ. In my fourth semester of Bible College, I had a mental and spiritual break down. Many issues caused the trial but one reality drove me into the darkness—I doubted and questioned God's goodness. In the midst of what was one of the strongest times of depression, I wasn't even sure if the Lord loved me anymore. I believed in the atoning work of Christ but I could not fight sin. I longed for the Spirit's presence but I was empty. During this time, I entered into a season of sin and despair until I saw the beauty of the Risen Christ in His Word. The Lord reassured my soul and cultivated my identity in Christ.

As a pastor, I have counseled individuals who have struggled in their Christian faith just like I have in the past. What I've come to realize is that many problems arise from a misguided understand regarding identity in Christ.

This small work is a passion project of sorts, a theological experience with the truth of Scripture, as well as, an extension of pastoral ministry. I know I'll walk through difficult times again; therefore, this book will also serve as a needed reminder to myself and to those who need encouragement in their personal walk with the Lord.

Michael Cooper
Mabank, Texas.

INTRODUCTION

Who am I?

This is the most important question you can ask yourself.

This is the question of identity. It is the most basic but foundational question that has been asked for centuries. This one question has been the center of philosophical, psychological, sociological, and theological discussions sparking a wide range of answers. At its root, it is both anthropological (what does it mean to be human) and existential (what does it mean to exist). "Who am I?" goes down to the very core of the human experience and existence. Simply put: Identity impacts who we are, what we believe, and how we live. Now let me flip that statement around: who we are, what we believe, and how we live also comprises our identity.

The question of identity drives who we are and how we view ourselves in this world. Many people define themselves by what they do. For example, if I were to ask you the question: "Who are you?" you could answer it with a description of your occupation. As such, I am a pastor of a local church. Some people define themselves by where they were raised. I was raised in Texas. Some appeal to their parents. My mom and dad are Dreama and Mike. But the question of identity goes deeper than just what you do, where you are from, or to whom you are related.

To complicate this, we live in a world where this question is becoming more difficult to answer. Identity confusion prevents many from experiencing the joys of this life.

Our culture has argued that identity is a social construct.[1] It's been said that race, sexuality, and gender are constructs set up by culture and can easily be changed. Moreover, these constructs create our identity as they define us. The categories of "male and female" are simple structures set up by a given society, so it is argued. In our broken world, these identity constructs are fluid; the answer to the identity question isn't black and white. Because they are not rooted in objective truth, we can redefine who we are. As some argue, "we need to let go of the need to define" ourselves so we can have the freedom to "choose any definition" we want.[2]

But the reality is the question of "Who am I?" is more than just an anthropological and existential exercise. The Biblical truth states that God is our Creator. The answer to the identity question, according to the Bible, begins with God. He has designed us for a purpose. He gives us identity. God has providentially created man and woman in His image (Genesis 1:26-28). In a world of identity confusion, this is why it is important to discover who you are in light of Jesus Christ.

People search for an identity, but the God of the Bible has already defined who we are. As we are created in His image, we are intrinsically beautiful. The Bible says we are fearfully and wonderfully made (Psalm 139:14). Though we are fallen, we know through the broken beauty this glorious reality of who God is. As John Calvin said, "There exists in the human mind and indeed by natural instinct, some sense of deity."[3] There is a 'sense of deity' calling out within us for the God of the universe. We long for a God-centered identity.

---

[1] http://criticalmediaproject.org/why-identity-matters/

[2] https://www.huffingtonpost.com/lorenz-sell/self-identity_b_3779389.html

[3] https://www.monergism.com/topics/calvin-john/sensus-divinitatis-sense-divinity

Cruciform Identity

The truth is, God is the foundation and fountain of all being and all beauty. God, who is objectively beautiful, is the very source of beauty in the universe.[4] While this sounds very abstract, this beauty is fully revealed in one simple act of love—the death and resurrection of Jesus. The only begotten Son, who died in the place of sinners and rose from the dead, demonstrates the fullest expression of God's beauty. There we see the heart of God. His heart is a heart of love that seeks to rescue people from the grasp of sin. When one trusts in the sacrifice of Christ, he becomes a "New Creation" (1 Corinthians 5:17). This is the beautiful truth of the Gospel.

But on a practical level, life doesn't always look this beautiful—even as Gospel shaped people. Rather, most times, life is actually a mess. We fail, we sin, and we fall. Honestly, sometimes we are just lucky to make it out of bed in the morning. But in Christ, it becomes a beautiful mess—the sacred cracking through the profane. It is beauty shining through our brokenness. While you may feel like you're limping towards Zion rather than marching, just know, you're going the right direction. The ups and downs of following Jesus can be overwhelming. Though at times I sense that I'm really not living my best life now or experiencing the Christian ideal, I have to remind myself of who I am in Christ. I get trapped in what I did or did not do rather than trusting in what Christ *did for me.*

Tucked in the middle of the New Testament, the Book of Romans stands the apex of Scripture. Romans 8 weaves the truth of beauty and identity together. In this mess of life, we need a reminder of who we are in Jesus and see the objective beauty of the Gospel that shines bright in Romans Chapter 8. We can say, according to God, the answer to the identity question is black and white. You are either in Christ or you are not. In this short work, I want to show you what the Bible says about your cruciform identity.

---

[4] This argument is drawn from Jonathan Edwards.

Michael Cooper

This book is for the "normal" Christian who struggles to understand who they are in Christ. The material contained in this work is not written for the academic but for those, like me, who have experienced an identity crisis. The overall theme of this book is the doctrine of "union with Christ" with Romans 8 as the foundation. The book is divided into two parts. In the first part, we will explore the theology of Romans 8 and related portions of Scripture. In the second part of this work, we will discuss some of the more practical issues related to union with Christ. The aim is to demonstrate how our union with Christ shapes our identity and our formation as believers.

Serving as a pastor, I'm convinced many personal issues can be resolved in the lives of believers by simply understanding their newfound identity in Christ. My prayer is that you'll realize who you are in Christ and understand your union with Him in a deeper way. May this book encourage your cruciform identity.

CHAPTER ONE

Identity Crisis

For me, it is anxiety. That is my "thorn in the flesh." It's that part of me that lurks in the shadows, waiting to pounce when I least expect it. Panic attacks, racing heart, and fear overwhelm my entire body and mind. But this doesn't define me. It is a part of me but not the whole.

For you it may not be anxiety, rather it could be your past. Maybe you come from a broken home with an abusive father. You wake up in fear, consumed by the pain of the past. Perhaps you are seeking to be defined by your job. You went to college, got that degree, and are now ready to earn a living. However, you've come to realize that the endless pursuit of money is a horrible way to live. You may be seeking purpose in a relationship. You are not complete until you find the "right one."

We all seek purpose, definition, and identity. These realities impact the entirety of our lives and they are fundamental to our existence. But the truth is often times we are looking in the wrong place to find the answers. In short, many of us are experiencing an identity crisis.

I'm sure you've heard of a mid-life crisis. It is often portrayed in movies with middle-aged men who aren't satisfied with life and attempt to discover who they are. Take for example, the 1999 blockbuster, *American Beauty*. The main character, Lester Burnham, played by Kevin Spacey explores the depths of his crisis through drug use and sexual fantasies until in the end, it kills him. Despite the taboo nature of this 1999 film, many in our culture are living in ways that reveal the truth of the movie: we must discover our identity, even if it's ugly to others but beautiful to us.

Of course, I believe the film missed the mark and it is a dark story of repressed sin. But I would suggest that *American Beauty* is a living parable for American life to the extent that people are longing for meaning, purpose, and identity in this life. This isn't something that happens just in the middle of life; it is a pursuit that begins when we are born.

A Broken Identity

I propose that our identity is broken. We've been looking for identity in all the wrong places and through all the wrong things. But our culture cannot provide us any real answers to our identity problem. Only God can do that.

The Bible begins with God, our good and loving Creator. He creates with a word. And at the apex of His creation in Genesis 1:26-28 the Bible states that God created humanity. Our first parents were called to be co-rulers with God over all that He had made. The original condition was "very good." God made us beautiful; furthermore, He gave us a purpose to know Him. However, our first parents listened to the voice of the serpent (the New Testament says this serpent was actually Satan). Their disobedience to God resulted in depravity. In the moment of this rebellion, they lost their identity.

According to Scripture, this brokenness has been passed down to us even today. Adam's fall scars our lives, leading to the complete corruption of our disposition. All of creation experienced the effects of the Fall until it broke the human heart. We are not morally good; rather, we are predisposed to sin because we are sinners. Sin corrupts our purpose and identity. It shatters our relationship with God and distorts how we live.

In the New Testament book of Romans, the Apostle Paul demonstrates that every person is condemned and deserves the wrath of God because of our sinful state (Romans

1:18-3:20). At the beginning of Paul's argument, lies the question of identity (Romans 1:18-32). Because of sin, we choose to worship creation rather than the Creator. But it doesn't stop there. The downward spiral of sin leads us to worship ourselves. Once we get tired of one idol, we move to the next. As Calvin states, "Our heart is a perpetual factor of idols." We are idol worshippers who suppress the truth. Our condition and identity are clear: we are "dead in our trespasses and sins" and "by nature children of wrath" (Ephesians 2:1-3).

As broken people we have two major issues. First there is an oppressive power called Sin. This power reigns over us (Romans 3:9-18). Our second issue is our individual sin(s). This is our broken morality and experience that stem from our idols. We are alienated and hostile in our actions (Colossians 1:21). The god of this age has blinded our minds from seeing the glory of gospel (2 Corinthians 4:4). This is not a good situation to be in.

Idols of Our Identity

The reign of Sin and our individual sin ultimately resulted in our desire for idols. Since we were created to worship God we intuitively know how to worship. But due to the Fall, dare I say, we have memorized the catechism of idolatry and participate in the liturgy of idol worship. We are desperate to worship something.

The tragic consequences of our idolatry have led to identity idols. These idols take the shape of our sinful hearts. Moreover, they seek to conform us into their image. A few of these identity idols:

- Family
- Occupation
- Relationships
- Sexuality/Gender
- Religion

- Nationality
- Money

These are just a few of the identity idols that we wrestle with in our search of purpose. But all of our idols will fall into three interrelated categories. Since the Fall broke our relationship with God, others, and even ourselves our identity idols emerge within those categories. First of all, our identity idols can be traced back to our desire to worship something other than God. Second, identity idols come from a yearning to have meaningful relationships with others. Third, these identity idols form as a result of our broken view of self. When we find ourselves in the middle of an identity crisis it can be traced back to one of the three.

The Cure for Our Identity Crisis

The worship of identity idols results in an identity crisis. Yet, the good news is, through the sacrifice of Christ we can discover our true identity and purpose. Our idols can be removed and a right relationship with God can be restored. The Apostle Paul makes it clear that one can be saved from God's wrath, and escape the consequences of sin by faith in Christ (Romans 5:6-11). This restoration of identity in Christ comes through our union with Christ. Here is where the argument of this book comes into focus: our union with Christ shapes our identity and spiritual formation. I call this our *cruciform identity*.

For many in the church world we've been taught the "ABCs" of salvation. A – accept that you are a sinner. B – believe that Jesus died for your sins. C – confess Him to be Lord.

While all of this is true the reduction of our understanding of salvation to the simple "ABCs" has left many in the church without a fully formed Christian identity. This is why union with Christ is a better way forward in determining our Christian faith and formation.

Yet for many Evangelical Christians this union with Christ idea may sound a bit strange, considering that most have never really explored this Biblical truth. But union with Christ is the way the Apostle Paul defined our Christian experience.

Union with Christ

Theologians have sought to trace the theme of union with Christ throughout Paul's letters. This doctrine has been for many Christians throughout church history the foundational doctrine for the Christian life. Listen to some of the voices from the past.

John Calvin:
...So long as we are without Christ and separated from him, nothing which he suffered and did for the salvation of the human race is of the least benefit to us. To communicate to us the blessings, which he received from the Father, he must become ours and dwell in us.[5]

The whole comes to this that the Holy Spirit is the bond by which Christ effectually binds us to Himself.[6]

Louis Berkof:
This union may be defined as that intimate, vital, and spiritual union between Christ and his people, in virtue of which He is the source of their life and strength, of their blessedness and salvation.[7]

---

[5] John Calvin, *Institutes of the Christian Religion* (Peabody MA: Hendrickson, 2008), 348-349.
[6] Calvin, *Institutes,* 349.
[7] Louis Berkhof, *Systematic Theology* (Grand Rapids: Eerdmans, 1976), 449.

John Murray:
Union with Christ is really the central truth of the whole doctrine of salvation not only in its application but also in its once-for-all accomplishment in the finished work of Christ. Indeed, the whole process of salvation has its origin in phase of union with Christ and salvation has in view the realization of other phases of union with Christ.[8]

It is the mysticism of communion with the one true and living God, and it is communion with the one true and living God because and only because it is communion with the three distinct persons of the Godhead in the strict particularity which belongs to each person in that grand economy of saving relationship to us.[9]

A.H. Strong:
Union with Christ is an organic union, in which we become members of Christ and partakers of his humanity, a vital union in which Christ's life becomes the dominating principle within us, it is a spiritual union that is a union whose source and author is the Spirit, an indissoluble union, a union which consistently with Christ's promise and grace can never be dissolved, an inscrutable union a mystical, however, only in the sense of surpassing in its intimacy and value any other union of souls which we know.[10]

James Leo Garrett:
Union is possible because of and on the basis of Jesus' saving death and resurrection. His saving work, not the created being of humans or human deeds of righteousness, is the

---

[8] Murray, *Redemption Accomplished and Applied*, 171.

[9] Murray, *Redemption Accomplished and Applied*, 171.

[10] Augustus Strong, *Systematic Theology* (Valley Forge: Judson Press, 1976), 795-808.

basis of the union. That union is with the risen and ascended Lord Jesus.[11]

James Boyce:
Union…determines our legal status on the same basis of His [Jesus], which revives and sustains, by the influence of His indwelling Spirit, our spiritual life from the fountain of His life, and which transforms our bodies and souls into the likeness of His glorified humanity.[12]

The Reality of Union with Christ

This idea of union with Christ is not a new idea. It is a Biblical idea that goes back to the very pen of Paul himself that wrote the heart of Jesus by the Spirit. So, let's flesh this out a bit. The Pauline theme of union with Christ is covenantal and experiential. What I mean by covenantal is simple. Union with Christ describes the saving benefits applied to the believer by the Spirit. By experiential I mean that the exalted Lord actually transforms our behavior.

Union with Christ is supernatural, spiritual, organic, and comprehensive.[13] For Paul, union with Christ is the web that holds our salvation and sanctification together.[14] It is important because union with Christ is the connecting point for nearly everything else the Apostle Paul says about justification by faith, penal substitution, and resurrection. In other words, the link between Paul's theological concepts is union with Christ.

So, what in the world does all this mean for you? I thought this was a book about Christian identity? You may be saying to yourself at this point, I just want to know how

---

[11] James Leo Garrett, *Systematic Theology: Biblical, Historical, and Evangelical,* vol II (Grand Rapids: Eerdmans, 1995), 336.
[12] James Boyce, *Abstract of Systematic Theology* (Hanford CA: Dulk Christian Foundation, reprint of 1887), 393.
[13] Demarest, *The Cross and Salvation*, 330-333.
[14] Campbell, *Paul and Union with Christ*, 442.

to be a Christian! I don't need all this theology stuff. Let me suggest that theology shapes our identity. The Bible says we are new creations *in Christ* (2 Corinthians 5:17). The question is what does it mean to be "in Christ?" *It really comes down to this—the concept of union with Christ is the lifeblood for all believers.*

This reality has very practical implications for us as followers of Jesus because our union with Christ shapes our moral identity.[15] Union with Jesus informs our choices, our goals, and our purpose. The Gospel claims that through Christ's death and resurrection we can have true life! We need to understand that who we are and what we do is no longer based on our performance; rather it is grounded in Christ's work for us.

This reality should liberate us. Being in Christ is what it means to be a Christian. Believing in Christ is being in union with Christ. According to the *Baker's Evangelical Dictionary*, Union with Christ is defined this way:

> *It is the present experience of the risen Christ indwelling the believer's heart by the Spirit…the Christian lives in vital union with Christ, expressing corporately the love of Christ personally appropriated by faith.*[16]

The cure for our identity crisis is to find our identity in Christ. If you are a believer you are in a real and living union with the Risen Christ. You and I have a cruciform identity. This means your present life is shaped by the gospel in the sense that you experience a spiritual death and resurrection in Christ. The rest of this book will seek to explore how this cruciform identity is created and how it shapes our lives. Our cruciform identity is created through our personal

---

[15] Grant Macaskill, *Living in Union with Christ: Paul's Gospel and Christian Moral Identity* (Grand Rapids: Baker, 2019).
[16] https://www.biblestudytools.com/dictionaries/bakers-evangelical-dictionary/union-with-christ.html

union with the living Christ by the Spirit and subsequently takes the form of Christ by the way we live.

Jesus is Lord

Before we dive deeper into our cruciform identity, we need to discuss the crucified message. Unfortunately, though in the American Christianity we have baptized the scandal of the cross in our moral civility. Roses have grown up around the instrument of death. As a result, the power of the cross is lost. In order to fully appreciate our cruciform identity, we need to flesh out some of the shocking aspects of the cross.

The Gospel proclaims that *Jesus is Lord.*[17] Those of us who live as witnesses of the Crucified Christ know all too well that mentioning the statement "Jesus is Lord" is a cultural "no-no." If you announce this you'll likely be labeled as "narrow-minded" or just simply someone who hasn't progressed far enough into the changing culture. Christians must, so the argument goes, stop being judgmental and be more inclusive of others. It is unfortunate that many who claim to follow the Crucified One have bought into that argument. The word of the cross, which was once a scandalous proclamation, has been simply reduced to a civilized opinion.

The message of Christianity will cause an offense. The truth claims that Jesus Christ, the Lord of the world, died in the place of sinners on a cross and rose from the dead will ruffle the feathers of the secular world. I'm convinced one of the main reasons for this is to be honest is that the message of the cross is utter nonsense to those who don't believe the gospel. I've been asked countless times, "Do you *really* believe that Jesus died and rose from the dead?" As if by believing in that truth claim, I've traded my critical thinking skills for a kindergarten fairytale. To believe in this truth,

---

[17] See Scot McKnight, *The King Jesus Gospel: The Original Good New Revisited* (Grand Rapids: Zondervan, 2016).

however, doesn't require one to empty their mind. Instead, it will require one to surrender their preconceived ideas of power and wisdom.

Paul writes in 1 Corinthians 1:18, "For the word of the cross is folly to those who are perishing, but to us who are being saved it is the power of God." It is here that one begins to see the "madness" of the Christian message. Note that the "word of the cross" produces two effects: folly to the perishing and power of God to those being saved. This message by application puts all of humanity into two categories: those perishing and those being saved. The classification is determined by one's response to the message.

The first effect that is produced by the gospel is folly to the perishing. The context Paul is writing into is extremely important. The Apostle is writing to the churches in the city of Corinth. This city was as Leon Morris said, "intellectually alert, materially prosperous, but morally corrupt."[18] Greek wisdom and philosophy filled the minds of those walked the streets of Corinth. It is here where we must see the cultural conflict with the gospel. The message of the cross in the Greco-Roman culture was complete madness. While there may have been a few Greco-Roman stories about gods dying and rising again it was ludicrous to suggest that a god would die a criminal's death on a cross.

To advocate "that the one pre-existent Son of the One True God, had appeared in very recent times in the out-of-the-way Galilee as a member of the obscure people of the Jews, and even worse, had died the death of a common criminal on the cross, could only be regarded as a sign of madness."[19] The cross is a complete paradox. It doesn't make any sense to those who are perishing. To paraphrase it this way; the message of the cross is considered insane by

---

[18] Leon Morris, *1 Corinthians* (Downers Grove: InterVarsity Press: 1985), 22.
[19] Martin Hengel, *Crucifixion* (Philadelphia: Fortress Press, 1977), 6-7.

those who don't believe. This is why the message of the cross is hard for people to believe. Why in the world would God send His One and Only Son to die on a cross? It is this very point that circumvents our understanding of God and the way He reveals Himself to the world. You see the cross is the highest revelation of God's wisdom, which stands in opposition to the wisdom of the world.

The cross challenges our understanding of power, wisdom, and identity. In a world that prides itself on human reasoning and strength, the cross of Christ pushes against those ideas, redefining what true wisdom and power actually look like. It is in the message of the cross that the power of God is revealed. David Garland explains, "In this case, 'power', refers to the effectiveness of the cross to make God known to humankind, to accomplish salvation, to defeat evil, and to transform lives and values."[20] This salvation wrought in the death of Jesus reveals God's power and wisdom. The question is asked, "Why in the world would God reveal Himself this way?" The answer is simple: God is wiser and stronger than us.

The reality is as sophisticated and relational humans, we seek to save ourselves a different way, a way that doesn't involve a bloody naked man on a cross. We would prefer a more civilized savior, one made in our own likeness. We would write and distribute our tracts proclaiming to all that good moral deeds and tolerance are the requirements for salvation. This is the wise thing to do. That wouldn't offend anyone. That message is more inclusive.

Yet it is through the foolishness of the cross that God is shown wiser than man. The weakness of God on the cross demonstrates He is stronger than any man. We could say that God has "outsmarted" all of humanity by revealing His wisdom and power through the death of His Son on the cross. As we attempt to think of a better way to save

---

[20] David Garland, *1 Corinthians*, New American Commentary Series (Grand Rapids: Baker, 2003), 62.

ourselves, God has already provided the most powerful instrument of deliverance. The symbol that was once a scandal has now become the symbol of salvation.

By Christ taking upon Himself the wrath of God, the sins of His people, and dying in their place, He revealed, His divine rescue mission for the world. The Crucified Christ redefines His people's understanding of God and the way He works in the world. The all-supreme Son of God condescended to the lowest point of humiliation possible—dying on a cross in the place of sinners. The power and the wisdom of God are revealed in the Crucified Christ.

But this Crucified Christ did not remain dead. The fundamental claim of Christianity is that Jesus was raised from the dead. The Apostle Paul states that if Christ is not raised, then we are dead in our sins (1 Corinthians 15:15-19). On the Sunday following Good Friday, Jesus came out of the tomb. The Christian Gospel announces that this Crucified and Risen One is the Exalted Lord. Jesus is currently enthroned in heaven and reigning over His people.

This message shapes who we are. As the world attempts to discover identity and purpose through idolatry the Gospel declares that the only way to discover true identity and purpose is through Jesus. The Gospel is the power that saves us. But it is also that message that brings us into union with Christ. It is upon this foundation that we begin to explore this profound truth concerning our cruciform identity.

CHAPTER TWO

Cruciform Identity and the Cross

If you were to walk into an ordinary church on any given Sunday the chances are great that you'd see a cross. It may hang over the baptismal pool, on a wall, or it might be on the front of the pulpit. Yet even though you may see a cross, you might not hear about the cross. So, let's be clear up front. At the heart of this book's proclamation stands a cross. If we are to understand anything about our cruciform identity in union with the Lord, we must understand that the cross is at the center of our faith. As we journey together in this work, we do so with a vision of the cross that shapes our entire existence. The cross creates our cruciform identity.

There is No Condemnation for Those in Christ

> *Therefore, there is now no condemnation for those in Christ Jesus.* Romans 8:1

This profound statement comes in the middle of Paul's letter to the Romans. Even more this one verse stands at the climax of an argument that Paul has been building since the beginning of his letter. As discussed in chapter 1 we saw that we are sinners in need of salvation. The wrath of God threatens our existence. We are condemned because of our rebellion. Yet in Christ there is salvation. But there is an issue: We still sin even after we come into union with Christ (Romans 7:14-25).

Shocking, right? We are still living east of Eden and experience the consequences of Adam's rebellion even as we are in Christ. Our identity ebbs and flows even while we sing "Amazing Grace" on Sunday mornings. There are times in our lives that sin wars within us, seeking to destroy us. Sin is our great enemy. It is an internal terrorist. At times our sin causes us to doubt and live in despair. Fear takes ahold of us. Our faith shakes. We cry out, "What a wretched man I am!" But this is why the cross of Christ is so important. It is finished! Our faith is not grounded in what we do, rather it is grounded in what Christ has already accomplished. In Christ our identity is secure because of the cross. The saving death of Jesus is the solid rock upon which our union with Him stands.

This is the apex of Biblical truth and the foundation of our identity in Jesus. Apart from Christ we are condemned. Our sin bears witness against us. The idea of condemnation carries with it the judicial pronouncement of "guilty" upon a person. Yet here is the amazing reality. Even though justified people wrestle with sin (Romans 7) there is still no condemnation in Christ. People like you and I, who are set right with God by faith in Jesus, no longer have the verdict of guilty hanging over our heads. Though you may sense guilt as a result of your past or even present sin, there is absolutely no condemnation for those in Christ. Think about it for a moment. Your whole life apart from Christ was one of guilt and shame. But in Christ, you are not condemned. You are free!

The work of Christ grounds our union with Him. This "no condemnation" is the counterpart to justification in Romans 5:1. Since we are justified (set right with God), we are not condemned (no longer guilty). What does this mean? Very simply no condemnation means that God doesn't hold our sin against us anymore. No condemnation means we are treated as innocent. No condemnation means our sins are forgiven. This is all because of Christ and our union with the Living Lord.

Freedom from the Power of Sin

The beauty of this truth found in Romans 8:1 is supported by two reasons. First: *The law of the Spirit of Life in Christ Jesus has set you free from the law of sin and death* (Romans 8:2). There exists a law that wages war against us. It's a law that comes before us and will continue after our bodies are put in the ground. It's the law of "sin and death." This law does not free people, rather it binds us. It makes us its slave. As broken humans we live under the oppressive power of Sin.

Sin is the power that makes humanity forget that we are created in the image of God and prevents us from depending upon God.[21] It is the dominant power that drives us to live for ourselves. The power of Sin compels us towards idolatry and misguided worship. Sin creates within us individual sins, which is immoral living.[22] This tyrannical dictator called Sin makes us bow down to idols. Therefore, the law of "sin and death" is the law that says, "If you sin, you will surely die" (paraphrase of Genesis 2:17).

Yet according to the Bible, we have been freed from this law by a greater law, namely the law of the Spirit of Life. The New Covenant promises that the New Law supersedes the former. Spiritually, we were dead and now made alive in Christ (Ephesians 2:4-7). The Spirit of Life proves His resurrection power by liberating us from the law that once chained us. So, my friend, if you are in Christ, we can say that we have been freed from the power of sin. We are no longer bound to our sin and no longer its slave (Romans 6:1-4). We don't have to obey the master anymore. We have been removed from the realm of sin and enter into the realm of freedom. We are not condemned because the Spirit has

---

[21] James D.G. Dunn, *The Theology of Paul the Apostle* (Grand Rapids: Eerdmans, 1998), 112.
[22] Dunn, *The Theology of Paul*, 114-124.

freed us from the power of sin. Charles Wesley captures this truth in the great hymn, *And Can It Be*:

> *Long my imprisoned spirit lay*
> *Fast bound in sin and nature's night*
> *Thine eye diffused a quick'ning ray*
> *I woke, the dungeon flamed with light*
> *My chains fell off, my heart was free*
> *I rose, went forth and followed Thee!*[23]

Freedom from the Penalty of Sin

But the Bible also states that something else took place. The second reason that there is no condemnation is because God frees us from the penalty of sin. The Scripture says, "He condemned sin in the flesh by sending his own Son in the likeness of sinful flesh as a sin offering." (Romans 8:3). The Son was condemned in our place as a sin offering. Jesus, the one who knew no sin became sin for us (1 Corinthians 5:21). Since Christ was condemned in my place, I am no longer condemned in the eyes of God. Since Jesus, God in the flesh, was condemned I am no longer treated as a criminal.

On December 7th, 1982, the state of Texas performed the first lethal injection in the USA. A deadly combination of liquid entered into the veins of the inmate inducing unconsciousness, then causing muscle paralysis and respiratory arrest, and then stopping the heart.[24] The reality is we are all condemned because of our sin. We all deserve the lethal dose of God's judgment. Instead, the Son took our place. The Son received our punishment. He took our lethal injection. He was treated as a criminal. He was condemned. As the late hymn writer put it:

---

[23] https://hymnary.org/text/and_can_it_be_that_i_should_gain
[24] http://www.nytimes.com/1982/12/07/us/technician-executes-murderer-in-texas-by-lethal-injection.html

Bearing shame and scoffing rude,
In my place condemned He stood;
Sealed my pardon with His blood.
Hallelujah! What a Savior![25]

The Cross of Christ: Penal Substitution

As we look at the cross to discover our identity, we need to explore its theology. We can rightly define the atonement as "penal substitution." Jesus bore the penalty we rightly deserve. He died in our place and He atoned for our sins. By faith in Jesus our guilt became His and we receive His righteousness.[26] His death on our behalf secures our faith union with Him. Our newfound identity is imprinted with the cross.

Romans 8:1 shows us that Christ became our legal substitute and paid the penalty for our sins, which is death. This is penal substitution written in large letters.[27] This is the great transaction: Jesus, the innocent one, was treated as the guilty one so that guilty ones, like you and I, can be treated as innocent. Jesus took the sting of Sin and drank its deadly poison.

Yet this profound reality of death and union needs to be looked at in more detail if we are to understand its impact personally. The doctrine of penal substitution states "that God gave Himself in the person of his Son to suffer *instead of us* the death, punishment and curse due to fallen humanity as the *penalty for sin.*"[28] Jesus suffered as a substitute in the

---

[25] http://www.hymntime.com/tch/htm/h/a/l/halwasav.htm
[26] Wayne Grudem, *Systematic Theology* (Grand Rapids: Zondervan, 2000), pg. 579.
[27] Robert A. Peterson, *Salvation Accomplished by the Son: The Work of Christ* (Wheaton: Crossway, 2012), pg. 380.
[28] Steve Jeffery, Michael Ovey, Andrew Sach, *Pierced for Our Transgressions: Rediscovering the Glory of Penal Substitution* (Wheaton: Crossway, 2007), 21. Emphasis is mine in order to highlight the two primary theological components of this view.

place of sinners and He suffered the penalty of human sin, which is death on the cross. J.I. Packer claims that the atoning work of Jesus gives full expression to the justice of God in relationship to human sin while simultaneously revealing the depths of God's love for humanity.[29]

Jesus acted as a willing substitute in the place of sinners on the cross. The very idea of a "substitute" is expressed in the New Testament, specifically with the phrases, 'Christ died for us", "Christ redeemed us…having become a curse for us", and "to give His life a random for many."[30] Biblically the reason is because a fallen humanity is under the reign of sin (Romans 3:9) and is internally corrupted by sins (Romans 1:18-32). At the heart of substitution is the reality that the One who knew no sin, was made to be sin *in our place* (2 Corinthians 5:21).[31] To say that Jesus died "in the place" of sinners does not mean that Jesus actually became a sinner on the cross. Jesus did not deserve to die since He was innocent. Rather He suffered for sinners as the "covenant representative and substitute."[32] The act is also described as 'penal', meaning penalty.[33] Scripture states that the wages of sin is death (Romans 6:23). Since God is holy,

---

[29] J.I. Packer, "What Did the Cross Achieve: The Logic of Penal Substitution" in *In My Place Condemned He Stood: Celebrating the Glory of the Atonement*, ed. J.I. Packer and Mark Dever (Wheaton, Crossway, 2007), 53-81.

[30] Packer, "What Did the Cross Achieve," 69. Also see Simon Gathercole, *Defending Substitution: An Essay on Atonement in Paul* (Grand Rapids: Baker Academic, 2015), 15.

[31] Bruce Demarest, *The Cross and Salvation: The Doctrine of Salvation*, Foundations of Evangelical Theology, ed. John S. Feinberg (Wheaton: Crossway, 1997), 174.

[32] Stephen J. Wellum, *Christ Alone: The Uniqueness of Jesus as Savior*, The 5 Solas Series, ed. Matthew Barrett (Grand Rapids: Zondervan, 2017), 210.

[33] Packer, "What Did the Cross Achieve", 77.

Cruciform Identity and the Cross

He must punish sin. Jesus paid the exact penalty for human rebellion, namely death.[34]

There is a dilemma that can be seen in Romans 1:18-3:20: How can God judge the evil of human sin (justice) and save sinners (mercy) without compromising His character? These two truths of God's justice and mercy seem to be in conflict. Enter Romans 3:21-26!

Romans 3:21-26 functions as the "main principle paragraph" of Romans.[35] To say it another way, it is the most important paragraph in the whole book! There are two major points in Romans 3:21-26.[36] The first major claim is found in v. 21-24: *God declares sinners righteous through their personal faith in Jesus* while the second major claim is in v. 25-26: *God can declare sinners righteous while maintaining his righteousness.*[37]

Romans 3:21-26 shows us that Jesus bore the wrath of God in the place of sinners because of the demands of God's justice against sin. He became a "propitiation" for sin. When you read this in your Bible you should interpret "propitiation" as a "wrath-bearing" sacrifice. In this way, God remains just and is able to justify those who have faith in Christ (Romans 3:26) since His wrath has been placated in Christ's death. God judges human sin in the body of Christ, and only then is He able to justify sinners by extending mercy to those who trust in Christ. This is because those who trust in Christ are brought into union with Him. We

---

[34] Steve Jeffery, Michael Ovey, Andrew Sach, *Pierced for Our Transgressions*, 121-123.
[35] David Allen, *The Atonement: A Biblical, Theological, and Historical Study of the Cross of Christ* (Nashville: Broadman and Holman, 2019), 75. Also see Ellis W. Deibler, *A Semantic and Structural Analysis of Romans*, Semantic and Structural Analyses Series (Dallas: Summer Institute of Linguistics, 1988), 93-94. I'm indebted to Dr. Roy Metts, Greek professor at Criswell College for exposing me to discourse analysis.
[36] Allen, *The Atonement*, 76.
[37] Allen, *The Atonement*, 76-77.

receive His righteousness as we trust in Him by faith. This union extends to us the saving benefits of justification. Through the death of Jesus, God maintains His moral integrity as God and is subsequently able to set sinners right with Himself.[38]

The Divine Substitute

What makes penal substitution "work" really comes down to the identity of the Substitute. Who died on the cross? If Jesus was merely an innocent peasant from first century Palestine, then the cross could never save. But Paul says that the Word of the cross has power to those who believe (1 Corinthians 1:18). How does the cross of Christ truly save?

If we take the New Testament seriously, we must see that Jesus was God the Son Incarnate. He was fully God and fully man. This God-Man was the One crucified. The punishment for sin—death—is satisfied in Christ (The Divine Son) in the place of sinners. To say it more plainly: *God in Christ substituted Himself on the cross*. As John Stott says, "God through Christ substituted Himself for us. Divine love triumphed over divine wrath by a divine self-sacrifice."[39]

It was God in Christ who was the Substitute. God was crucified! As Paul says, God was in Christ reconciling the world to Himself (2 Corinthians 5:17-21). It was God who turned His own wrath in upon Himself in the person of the Son. Dare I say it this way: God condemned Himself in the place of sinners. God the Son incarnate paid the full price for sin, death itself. It was God through Christ who satisfies His own demands for human sin.[40] Since it was God in Christ who paid the penalty for our sin and appeased His

---

[38] Robert A. Peterson, *Salvation Accomplished by the Son: The Work of Christ* (Wheaton, Crossway, 2012), 87.
[39] John Stott, *The Cross of Christ* (Downer Groves: IVP, 1986), 158-159.
[40] Wellum, *Christ Alone*, 212.

own wrath against sin, there is no condemnation for those who have faith in the Substitute. The Biblical gospel proclaims that God was satisfying Himself by substituting Himself for us.[41]

The Suffering and Victory of God

What is happening in the Son's work on the cross is beyond our mere comprehension. As fallen humans we are grasping for straws, attempting to understand the depths of the cross. But the New Testament is abundantly clear that it was God in the person of the Son who willingly took upon Himself the vileness of our broken humanity.[42]

But we also must recognize that in the cross we see the triumph of God over the powers. We must remember that Sin and our sins are the problem. Through the death of Jesus Christ, we see His victory over sin, Satan, and death through His penal substitutionary sacrifice for sinners. You and I need to see the cross as a victorious sacrifice. Jesus simultaneously defeats Satan, reveals the Kingdom of God, and demonstrates the love of God by experiencing the penalty of human sin because He died as a substitute. In order words Christ is victorious through His work on the cross.[43] Christ frees us from the power of Sin by dying in our place for our sin.

Paul writes in Galatians 1:3-4 that Jesus Christ "gave Himself for our sins to rescue us from the present evil age." Jesus willingly gave Himself in the place of our sins, taking the sin of humanity on Himself. The purpose for His death was to rescue a fallen humanity from the present evil age, an age comprised of death, sin, and Satanic opposition. In

---

[41] Stott, *The Cross of Christ*, 160.

[42] Fleming Rutledge, *The Crucifixion: Understanding the Death of Jesus Christ* (Grand Rapids: Eerdmans, 2015), 93.

[43] Jeremy Treat, *The Crucified King: Atonement and Kingdom in Biblical and Systematic Theology* (Grand Rapids, MI: Zondervan, 2014), 208.

Paul's writings the "present evil age" is dominated by Satanic corruption.[44] This phrase indicates that there is both a substitution for sins and deliverance from oppression. In the mind of the Apostle Paul both need to occur in order for humanity to be saved.

Consider Colossians 2:13-15, which claims that humanity was "dead in trespasses" but Jesus "forgave us all our trespasses." Christ can forgive us through His death. But we see specifically that He "erased the certificate of debt...by nailing it to the cross." Explicitly the text indicates that Jesus erased the legal demands of sins and implicitly claims that Jesus satisfied the punishment deserved by sin.[45] The Bible shows us result of this work: "He disarmed the rulers and authorities and disgraced them publicly, he triumphed over them in Him." Once again, Paul is tying together the ideas of substitution and triumph through His redemptive work on the cross.

This parallels the Apostle's words in Colossians 1:13-14. God "rescued us from the domain of darkness and transferred us into the kingdom of the Son He loves." Note the kingdom language used in connection with the atonement. Paul explains how this occurred in the next phrase, "In Him we have redemption, the forgiveness of sins." In Colossians 1:22, Paul states, "He has reconciled you by His physical body through His death…" The death of Jesus accomplished reconciliation and redemption that results in the forgiveness of sins. This act involves the transferal of a believing humanity from one domain to another. Clearly the ideas of deliverance from dark oppression and redemption from sin's oppression are tied together in Colossians.

While there are many more passages that discuss this truth, we must rest in the beauty of the cross. Jesus dies as a substitute in the place of sinners and is victorious over

---

[44] George Eldon Ladd, *A Theology of the New Testament*, Revised Edition (Grand Rapids: Eerdmans, 1993), 402-403.
[45] Treat, *The Crucified King*, 206.

Satan/Sin. The Savior is victorious over Satan by suffering vicariously for sinners.[46] Christ wins by dying!

The Revelation of God's Love

But what is the point to all of this cross stuff and how does it affect our identity? Simply put: the cross is the full demonstration of God's love for us and this is the ground of our identity. In Romans 5:6-11 we discover that God proves His love for us through the death of Christ in our place. In Romans 5:6, we see who we are—we were helpless. Without Christ we are spiritually weak, helpless, and sick. Also, the Bible says we are ungodly. We are sinful. We have broken God's law and stand under His judgment.

But the Bible says at the right time when we were powerless and unable to save ourselves, Christ died for us. At the moment in our weakness and sin sick state, God through Christ went to the cross to die for us. (Romans 5:7) The extent of God's love is shown in the fact that Jesus didn't die for good people or righteous people. Rather God's love is seen in Christ dying in the place of sinners, His enemies.

The profound truth of the cross is this: Christ did not wait for us to clean ourselves up in order to save us. Jesus died *while we were sinners*. New Testament scholar Leon Morris writes,

> *He loves because of what He is, not because of what we are. There is nothing in sinners to call forth the love of God. But He does love us, as the cross so plainly shows Christ died for us comes at the end with impressive simplicity. It is a succinct statement of the essence of the Christian message.*[47]

---

[46] Treat, *The Crucified King*, 224.
[47] Leon Morris, *The Letter to the Romans*, The Pillar New Testament Commentary (Grand Rapids: Eerdmans, 1998), 224.

Since God has proven His love for us through the death of Jesus we are now saved from wrath and we are now reconciled to God. We were once enemies of God because of our sin. We stood in rebellion against Him. The idea of reconciliation means that now through faith in Jesus we are brought into a friendly relationship with God. Our response should be very simple: Rejoice! The cross demonstrates that God indeed loves us. We've been saved from wrath and we are now in a relationship with God through Christ. The dying Savior rescues us from wrath, sin, and Satan because of His love.

Union with Christ and the Cross

This cross talk impacts the way we think about our identity. The cross of Christ creates our cruciform identity and establishes the foundation of love for our lives. In a world where we struggle with sin inside and outside of us it is easy to fall into despair. It can become overwhelming to see the bitter brokenness of our own hearts and the cruel tragedy of Sin's reign. But there stands the cross. The King reigns for the tree![48]

The cross of Christ is the basis for our union with Christ and the fundamental element that shapes our identity. There is no condemnation for those united to the One who was condemned in our place. My brother and sister, if you are in Christ, you are free! Our identity as free men and women flows from the saving death of God's own Son. Let's not continue to limp through life with the ball and chain of condemnation. We exist as free people, saved from the grip of Sin and our sin.

In the cross of Christ, He is victorious over the power of Sin and He rectifies our individual sin issue. He defeats Satan and silences his demons. The cross creates our cruciform identity. As we exist in a Living union with the

---

[48] Lesslie Newbigin, *Foolishness to the Greeks: The Gospel and Western Culture* (Grand Rapids: Eerdmans, 1986), 99.

Cruciform Identity and the Cross

crucified Christ, our lingering guilt and shame melt away by the all-consuming fire of the cross. When we survey the cross, we grasp the price of our union.

Because of our union we are justified.[49] Your justification was purchased by His death. Our cruciform identity is a justified reality. Let's live with our eyes on the cross because the Spirit has imprinted the cross on our hearts. In chapter two we will discuss the Spirit's role in our union with Christ and how He transforms our identity.

---

[49] Marcus Peter Johnson, *One with Christ: An Evangelical Theology of Salvation* (Wheaton: Crossway, 2013), 88.

CHAPTER THREE

Cruciform Identity and the Spirit

At my parents' house growing up, we had a pear tree. I wasn't a huge fan of pears so it didn't bother me much when it stopped producing the fruit. The frustrating part about a dead tree was cleaning up the rotten fruit on the ground. This poor tree was a fruitless tree. It was worthless. The old tree was simply in the way. It failed to do the exact thing it was created to do. Apart from Christ, we are just like that fruitless tree. Yet living in union with Jesus grants us the opportunity to experience the Fruit Producer Himself—the Holy Spirit. The Spirit of God binds our hearts to Christ and cultivates our cruciform identity.

Who is the Spirit?

The Spirit of God is often misunderstood. But we must be clear. The Spirit is the personal presence of Christ. In the moment when we trusted in Christ, we received the Spirit of God and were sealed (Ephesians 1:14). The Holy Spirit is not an "it" or a nebulous energy. Rather, the Spirit is a person. He is the resurrected presence of Jesus dwelling within us.

Rankin Wilbourne in his book, *Union with Christ*, states,

> *The Spirit is the real, living bond between Jesus and us. Having the Spirit…is the equivalent, indeed the very mode, of having the incarnate, obedient, crucified, resurrected, and exalted Christ*

indwelling us so that we are united to Him as He is united to the Father.[50]

Furthermore, the Spirit of God is the fulfillment of God's promises to be with His people.[51] With this truth in mind, the Bible explains the role of the Spirit in our lives. Let's explore how the Spirit empowers us to overcome the flesh.

As we continue to look at Romans 8, we should notice in verse 4 that we now possess the ability to live the life that God designed us to live by the Spirit. The Bible says, "In order that the law's requirements would be fulfilled in us." Verse 4 indicates the purpose of the "not condemned" reality. But notice this truth; namely, the law's requirements would be fulfilled in us. This means we have the ability to live according to God's law and fulfill what He desires us to do by the power of the Spirit. The phrase *"who do not walk according to the flesh but according to the Spirit"* is an important distinction. The way we can live the life that pleases God is only by the Spirit. At this juncture we need to discuss the difference between the "flesh" and the Spirit.

The 4 Effects of the Flesh

In the New Testament we find language of the Spirit and the flesh. In Romans 8:4, Paul says we can fulfill the Law's requirements if we walk by the Spirit and not the flesh. But let's be honest. The language of "walking by the Spirit and walking by the flesh" can be pretty confusing. But the Apostle Paul helps us define what this actually means in Romans 8:5-8.

Paul says that those who walk by the flesh have their minds on the flesh. This fleshly mindset leads to death. The

---

[50] Rankin Wilbourne, *Union with Christ* (Colorado Springs: David C. Cook, 2016), pg. 51.
[51] Gordon Fee, *God's Empowering Presence: The Holy Spirit in the Letters of Paul* (Grand Rapids: Baker, 2011), 845.

flesh cannot submit to God and it cannot please God (Romans 8:5-8). Now "the flesh" that Paul is talking about is not the flesh on your body (e.g. skin).

Rather, Paul is speaking about the "old way of life." It is the realm of existence that runs contrary to God. New Testament scholar Douglas Moo, states,

> *To walk according to the flesh is to have one's life determined and directed by the values of this world, the world in rebellion against God. To walk according to the Spirit on the other hand, is to live under the control and according to the values of the new age created and dominated by God's Spirit, two different realms of existence. You are either of the Spirit or of the flesh.*[52]

I'm sure you've seen the cartoon where the main character has an angel and a demon perched on each shoulder arguing about the best way to live. Unfortunately, many Christians have this idea about themselves as if there are two natures dwelling inside of them (one good and one bad). But the Bible doesn't present a "two nature" theology, at least not here in Romans 8. The distinction between the flesh and the Spirit has to do with the present evil age and the age to come. The old age (the flesh = present evil age) is passing away while the new age (the Spirit = age to come) is already present. But since we live between the already and the not yet, we still must learn to walk by the Spirit as opposed to the flesh.[53]

The Bible makes it clear that one is either of the Spirit or of the flesh. There is no grey area when it comes to walking in the flesh or the Spirit. As a believer, you can't have one foot in the realm of the Spirit and one foot in the realm of the flesh.

---

[52] Douglas Moo, *NICNT: The Epistle to the Romans* (Grand Rapids: Eerdmans, 1996), pg. 485.

[53] Fee, *God's Empowering Presence*, 822.

You can't live the way God wants if you are *in the flesh*. The flesh is death but the Sprit is life. The flesh is unable to submit to God and it cannot please God. Before you trusted in Jesus, you were in the flesh. You were consumed by it, and as a result, you could not submit to God nor could you please God. In your unregenerate state, you were hostile to God (Colossians 1:20-22). But now, in Christ, you have been freed from the age of the flesh since the Spirit frees from the power of sin (Romans 8:2).

Practically, how do you know if you are still in the flesh?

- Are you still bound by your sin?
- Do you find it difficult to submit to God's Word?
- Are you hostile to the things of God?
- Is your mindset upon the things of the flesh (lust of flesh, lust of eyes, pride of life see 1 John 2:15-17)?

We must remember as fallen people, we still sin. Although we have received a new nature by the Spirit, we are still tempted to walk according to the way of the flesh. It's as if the kingdom of the flesh is calling out to us, seeking to woo us back into the old patterns of life. However, the Spirit's power is stronger than the flesh. We can wage war against the flesh. This is due to the fact that the Spirit freed us from the law of sin and death. This law no longer binds us!

The 4 Benefits of the Spirit

Romans 8:9-11 shows us that there are four benefits of the Spirit: The Spirit lives in you, the Spirit is the sign that we belong to Christ, the Spirit gives life, and the Spirit will raise you up on the last day. The Spirit of the Living God provides you life because He lives within you now.

Cruciform Identity and the Spirit

Let's be clear: The Spirit is not energy or some mysterious source of power. Rather, the Spirit is the third person of the Trinity. The Spirit is a person that dwells within us once we believe in Christ. In other words, we are connected to the Life source (Jesus) by the Spirit. The same Spirit that raised Christ from the dead now dwells in us and will give life to our mortal bodies. This means that one day, you will die. Your heart will stop beating. The blood will stop flowing. Your body will decay. But the Spirit will give you life on the last day, by raising you from the dead.

So, what is the sign that you have the Spirit?

- Do you desire the things of God?
- Do you seek to grow in holiness?
- Do you sense conviction when you sin?
- Is there liberation from sin?

The Spirit of God does not promote chaos or fear. Rather, the Spirit brings peace and order. This is what we need in a world of chaos and fear. The Spirit brings inner peace and helps us overcome sin. This is life lived by the Spirit.

Live According to the Spirit and Not the Flesh

The life defined by the Spirit is not obligated to live according to the flesh. This means we are not in "debt" to the flesh. At one point in time during our lives the only thing we could do is sin. But since you have been freed from sin's power and penalty, you don't have to live according to the flesh anymore. The reason is due to the fact that the flesh leads to death but the Spirit gives us the ability to put to death the flesh.

As the great puritan author John Owens stated, "Do you mortify? Do you make it your daily work? Be always at it while you live; cease not a day from this work; be killing sin or it will be killing you."[54]

Christian, you are not condemned. You are free to live the life God has designed you to live by the Spirit. Prior to being "in Christ" you did not have the ability to live such a beautiful life. However, you have a newfound identity. You are a brand-new person. As Paul would say elsewhere, you are a "new creation" (2 Corinthians 5:17-21). Your identity is in Christ and Him alone. You were stuck in your sin and unable to function. But since the Spirit has freed you from the power of sin and Christ has delivered you from the penalty of sin, my friend, you can walk in freedom. If you are attempting to live according to God's design in your own flesh, you are attempting to scale Mount Everest without oxygen. But by the Spirit you can journey up the mountain of the Christian life through faith in Christ.

God's Sons are Led by God's Spirit

The Spirit of God that binds us to Christ has a practical ministry in our lives. We can refer to this practical ministry of the Spirit as His activity.[55] First of all, the Spirit has a leading ministry (Romans 8:14). Everyone led by the Spirit is a child of God. Do you remember the contrast in the early section of Romans 8? Christians have the Spirit and are called to walk according to His power rather than the flesh. The realm of the Spirit and the flesh wage war against each other. Paul is drawing a contrast between believers and unbelievers—only God's children are led by God's Spirit.

If you believe in Jesus, the Spirit lives inside you. The Spirit makes the person of Christ "real" to you. In the Old Testament, the Spirit did not reside within the people of God individually. Instead the Spirit was given to prophets, priests, and kings. However, in the New Testament the

---

[54] John Owens, *The Mortification of Sin* (Carlisle Penn: Banner of Truth, 2004).

[55] Fee, *God's Empowering Presence*, 829-831.

Cruciform Identity and the Spirit

Spirit dwells in all believers. The Spirit joins us to the very life of Christ.[56] We are in Christ and Christ is in us by the Spirit.

Understanding this amazing truth, we see the Spirit's ministry of leading us. The proof that we are God's children is revealed in the fact that the Spirit leads us. What does this mean? I believe the "leading" of the Spirit is experienced in various ways. First, the Spirit leads us to understand the conviction of sin. The Spirit shows us our failures and then provides us the power to overcome them. Second, the Spirit illuminates the Word and shows us God's truth. As you read the Bible, the Spirit is leading you into truth. Next, the Spirit cultivates virtue. In Galatians 5:22-26, we see the fruit of the Spirit, which speaks about the way a Christian must live. The Spirit cultivates the fruit in our lives by building Christian character.

Do you remember the first time you heard the annoying voice of the GPS saying, "Turn left, go straight, make a U-turn?" Well, I remember it. As we were driving, the voice would squeak "redirecting" every time we veered off course. At the time, I was pretty sure that the expensive device had no idea where we were going on the back roads of East Texas. The truth is, the GPS kept me on track and without it, I'd probably still be lost. I had no idea where I was, but the GPS was leading me. In a deeper sense, without the Spirit we would be lost. The Spirit directs us and leads us into all truth. The Spirit is providing us the right way to go and leading us down that path of righteousness. The Spirit leads us so we must allow the Spirit to work in our lives.

---

[56] Fred Sanders, *The Deep Things of God: How the Trinity Changes Everything* (Wheaton: Crossway, 2010), pg. 59.

God's Children Have Received the Spirit of Adoption

As believers in Jesus, we did not receive a *Spirit of slavery*. The Spirit of slavery is referring to the fear of condemnation as a result of sin (Romans 6:15-23). Apart from Christ, we are slaves to sin. We are ruled by sin. Sin is our taskmaster and for the majority of our lives we obeyed its voice.

But we have received the *Spirit of Adoption*. As a pastor, I've had the opportunity to see many families walk through the adoption process. Standing there with a family from church receiving their new family member, provided insight into the spiritual truth of adoption. Much like adoption in the 21st century, spiritual adoption comes with various benefits. Think about it for a moment: As believers we have a Father. We have inherited full family rights as heirs. We also have legal protection, which specifically includes no separation (Romans 8:31-39). In Romans 8:15, it states that the Spirit of Adoption allows us to cry out: *Abba, Father*.

In the 1st century, kids in the home used the word "Abba." It was a term of affection, endearment, and love. It is much like how my two little girls call me "daddy." It was an informal term that carried affection. In the same way, we have the ability, by the power of the Spirit, to call out to our Heavenly Father who loves us. The truth is though; we live in a culture that is plagued with fatherlessness. Many grow up without fathers or if they do, some experience abusive fathers. My brother and sister, I am sorry you experienced this from the hands of your earthly father. Please know that our Heavenly Father is not abusive and He will never abandon us. He is patient, kind, and gentle. He loves us unconditionally. He proved this by sending His only Son to die for the sins of the world (John 3:16; Romans 5:8).

Once we understand the movement of the passage, we catch a glimpse into its application power. This is a rags-to-riches story. I want you to see it: you were once a slave to sin but now you are a child of the King! You have a

Heavenly Father who cares for you and you have the Spirit that leads you.

The Spirit Testifies that We Are God's Children

But the Spirit has another role, namely He *bears witness* with our spirit. This means that the Spirit of God confirms that we are God's children. It is important to understand that this "witness" is not a feeling but rather a deep sense of knowing.

Theologians call this *the internal testimony of the Spirit*. I would say that the internal testimony is a subjective experience of the Spirit that confirms the objective reality of the Word's Truthfulness about Christ and our relationship with Him. The late theologian R.C. Sproul writes the profound statement:

> *There is an internal testimony within the hearts of believers that assures them of God's fatherhood and preservation of them as His beloved sons and daughters. Note that the Spirit does not give testimony apart from His Word. Paul has to tell us that we are children of God, just as the Lord has always given an objective Word to His people through the prophets. The Spirit takes this external Word and confirms it internally. He provides subjective assurance that God's objective Word applies to us when we believe.*[57]

Many Christians struggle with the doctrine of assurance. They know their own failures by personal experience and in many cases, continue to struggle with past sins. But the Spirit is the guarantee of assurance. Do you sense a conviction of sin? Do you desire to know Christ more? Do you experience the prompting of the Spirit? When you read Scripture does your heart burn to know it more? These are all evidences of the Spirit and confirmation of assurance.

---

[57] https://www.ligonier.org/learn/devotionals/spirits-internal-witness/

This is the amazing truth: we are part of God's new creational family. We are heirs of God, meaning we share in the blessings of the Father, and we are co-heirs with Christ. This simply means that what Christ has is now ours by faith. But these benefits come at a cost. You see the pathway to glory isn't easy. Rather, suffering leads to glory.

Most times in life we desire ease and comfort. But the Christian life doesn't promise that, rather, it does promise us that if we follow Jesus we will walk in His footsteps. Suffering is a reality in the Christian experience (suffering is a major theme in Romans 8). You will suffer because you live in a fallen world.

This world is scarred by the Fall and you have been living East of Eden. As a result, suffering is part of life. However, for the Christian, we have a promise—the promise of a glorified state. You are not the sum total of your failures, sin, or suffering. In Christ the Spirit provides you personal assurance that you are God's treasure.

Union with Christ and the Spirit

In Christ we have the Spirit working within us, blessing us with the benefits of the Father, and conforming us into the image of Jesus. This is what we need because this is what's most beautiful. Our new identity in Christ provides us with real spiritual benefits from the Spirit. The Spirit cultivates our cruciform identity in several ways.

First the Spirit gives us the ability to walk in freedom. He empowers us to overcome personal sin that ties us to the age of the flesh. Second the Spirit ministers to us through His leading, adopting, and assuring purposes. This is because the Spirit is a person, the personal presence of Christ, and the empowering presence of God.[58] Because of Christ's work on the cross and the Spirit's work within us, we have all we need now and forever. The Spirit binds us to Christ, sealing an unbreakable bond to the Jesus.

---

[58] Fee, *God's Empowering Presence*, 5.

CHAPTER FOUR

Cruciform Identity and the Resurrection

There is a forward orientation within humanity. We are always trying to move forward, progress, and advance. Think about technological advancements for a moment. In 2007, the Apple iPhone was launched, creating a new path of smartphones and technology. A close friend at the time bought the new device. We sat around in awe for hours looking at the phone with our old flip phones in our pockets, embarrassed to pull them out. That advancement was a huge leap forward from years earlier. Instead of having to go to a desktop computer, that same technology was placed in your hand.

The late Apple CEO, Steve Jobs, believed that a person could have one device that could play music, make phone calls, and browse the Internet. He stated in his iPhone launch presentation, "Today, Apple is going to reinvent the phone."[59] This forward orientation was the first step into new technological developments. To put this into perspective, I remember when I was in the 1st grade seeing a desktop computer for the first time. And now my daughter is watching educational videos on my phone by my side as I write this chapter.

---

[59] YouTube video of the 2007 iPhone presentation: https://www.youtube.com/watch?v=vN4U5FqrOdQ

I'm convinced that this forward orientation is a deep-seated desire of humanity. It is part of our identity to look forward and beyond the present. We see where we are and we desire to move forward. Much like Steve Jobs, we desire that this world be "reinvented." We want to progress and grow. But we are stuck in the tension—wanting to move forward into the not yet but experiencing the brokenness of the already. I dare you to ask any person if they are truly satisfied with life, as we know it. I'm sure most would probably say something akin to "life could be better." But this "could be better life" is a subjective apologetic for the new world promised in Romans 8:18-27. There we find a powerful truth concerning the future and our hope for the resurrection.

Paul focuses here upon the future reality and how that impacts our present. The Christian tradition teaches us that the resurrection is a grand goal for the world and humanity. The fullness of it hasn't arrived yet. And here the Bible presents a clear truth about the future and we as believers have a front row seat for the end! The resurrection to come directs our cruciform identity.

Creation Groans for the Revelation of the Sons of God

> *The sufferings of this present time are not worth comparing with the glory that is going to be revealed to us.* Romans 8:18

What we are experiencing right now does not compare to what God has for us in the future. Let me say that this is indeed good news! Through the brokenness of our world there is a ray of hope in the resurrection. The Bible describes that future glory and how it impacts our lives now. While we are stuck in the tension, we recognize that this world will one day be renewed and reinvented. The beautiful reality becomes true for us by faith in Christ.

Cruciform Identity and the Resurrection

In this section of Romans 8, Paul begins by appealing to creation. You see creation itself waits for the final resurrection. The Bible says that creation eagerly awaits. The word used here for eagerly awaits (*apokaradokia*) presents a visible image. It's like a child stretching her neck out looking for her daddy coming home. This eager waiting will one day be complete when the sons of God are revealed. Creation is waiting for that one moment at the end of history when the children of God are revealed and experience the full restoration.

But again, here is the tension. The creation was subjected to the curse of the fall. The reason we have natural disasters is due to the fact that all of creation experienced the effects of the Fall. However, it was subjected *in hope*. The hope discussed here, is the hope of God's promise to restore the world to right. Creation will be set free from its bondage. New Testament scholar N.T. Wright states:

> *The New Testament invites us, then, to imagine a new world as a beautiful, healing community; to envisage it as a world vibrant with life and energy, incorruptible, beyond the reach of death and decay; to hold it in our mind's eye as a world reborn, set free from the slavery of corruption, free to be truly what it was made to be.*[60]

One day, creation itself will experience an exodus, liberation into a new freedom. Right now, though, creation is groaning with labor pains. It is longing for the fullness of restoration. The world is longing to be reborn.

My wife is the strongest woman I know and this was demonstrated in the birth of our children. The pain, agony, and suffering she experienced became almost unbearable until that doctor asked if she wanted an epidural. Up until that point Kailie refused, as she wanted to experience natural birth. But once the pain became so severe, she opted for

---

[60] N.T. Wright, *Evil and the Justice of God* (Downers Grove: InterVarsity Press, 2006), pg. 118.

relief (Let me just say if it were me, the epidural would have been the first thing I would have asked for). The labor pain went away allowing for an easy delivery. Unlike physical labor, creational labor doesn't have an epidural at this moment. There is nothing that can stop the pains of creation. The only reality that can stop it, is delivery, which is resurrection.

Some have been taught that at the end of time God is simply going to destroy the world as if creation does not matter. However, that is contrary to the Biblical teaching here. Creation will experience a new creation. Creation itself is groaning for the future. We see the inherent goodness of creation and the interconnectedness between creation and humanity. Humans were created to rule over creation but lost that right (Genesis 1:26-28). So, in the new world, through the resurrection, there will once again be the rightful rule of humanity over creation. This is why creation is groaning for the revelation of God's children. Creation needs humanity to rule over it, the way God intended.

We Groan for the Resurrection of the Body

As creation is longing for renewal, we groan for the resurrection. We are groaning for final adoption, which is the redemption of our bodies. This groaning is due to the brokenness around us and within us. We experience the tension of the "already and the not yet"—the already of the old world and the not yet of the new. Our groaning is for the resurrection. The hope of the New Testament is final resurrection from the dead. God has created humanity as body, soul, and spirit. So, the resurrection is the raising of a physical body from the grave.

Many of our old hymns speak about the afterlife. Take for example *I'll Fly Away* or *When We All Get to Heaven*. To a certain extent these beautiful songs are true and we should sing them with passion! However, our final hope is not a disembodied heaven but an embodied new earth

Cruciform Identity and the Resurrection

(Revelation 21:1-2). But why do we long for resurrection? As the last chapter discussed, the Spirit of God is the "sign" of a Christian. But Paul furthers his argument by stating that the Spirit is the first fruits or the down payment of a future reality. This is a pledge of a greater future.

My wife and I received a gift card to a nice steakhouse in Dallas. I'm pretty sure steak is our mutual love language so we were excited to jump at this opportunity. As we were looking up the menu online, we noticed that the steakhouse was known for its mac and cheese appetizer. Needless to say, mac and cheese is right behind steak on my favorite foods list. So, of course, when we arrived and were seated, we ordered the famous cheese covered noodles. Not knowing what to expect and paying a pretty penny, I was apprehensive about this mac and cheese. Let's just say, I'd pay double to experience that appetizer again. But think about this: if the appetizer was that good, what do you think the main course was like? To let you know, that steak melted in my mouth! In the same way, the goodness of the Spirit as our "appetizer" is pointing to a better "main course" of resurrection and new creation.

The resurrection provides us hope and it is in this hope, we are saved. Our hope is not dead but ALIVE! We don't see this hope quite yet but we know it is near because our hope is grounded in a Risen Savior! This means that the resurrection launched God's rescue plan. The Resurrection promises a renewed future for God's people and the world. Lastly, the Resurrection is evidence that God has not abandoned the world. And here we find the difference between hope and optimism! Optimism is blind wishful thinking. But hope is the promised guarantee that God will fulfill His promises.

In his book, *A New Heaven and a New Earth*, Middleton writes,

> *The first step in the process of redemption, therefore, is that the oppressors must be liberated from their own sin...but this*

> *redemption is not simply a matter of being released from bondage; there is an implied positive goal…the future redeemed exercise of human rule over the earth.*[61]

Once again, we see the interconnectedness between humanity and creation. In our groaning, we are longing for resurrection and renewal. And in that day, we will finally be released from bondage and enter into what we were created to be—rulers with God (see Genesis 1:26-27 and Revelation 20:1-8). This is our created purpose.

We are called to live in union with God and serve Him joyfully. This coming new world will make His purpose for our lives into a reality. And our future purpose is Jesus-shaped, as Dr. Russell Moore writes,

> *Jesus shows us the goal of the future—of our lives individually and congregationally, and of the galaxies and solar systems around us. We tend either to ignore the future, because we are so consumed in the drama of the here and now, or to see it as simply a continuation of our present lives, with our loved ones there, and sickness and death gone. But in Jesus we see a future that has continuity and discontinuity. In his resurrected life, Jesus has gone before us as a pioneer of the new creation.*[62]

The Spirit Groans Within Our Weakness

The flow of the text is important: all creation *groans* for the resurrection while we ourselves *groan* for renewal. But the passage also says that the Spirit *groans* in our weakness. The Spirit is groaning within us in the midst of our suffering and weakness. The Spirit of God within us is calling out for the new world. He is longing for the renewal of the universe. He is directing our attention to the future.

---

[61] J. Richard Middleton, *A New Heaven and a New Earth: Reclaiming Biblical Eschatology* (Grand Rapids: Baker, 2014), pg. 160.
[62] https://www.christianitytoday.com/ct/2012/february/jesus-afterlife.html

Cruciform Identity and the Resurrection

We may experience times when the brokenness of this present world may be too much for us, causing us to struggle in prayer. However, we trust that the Spirit is communicating to the Son who in turn speaks to the Father for us. This deep and mysterious experience is too much to discuss here in this work, however, it is important to note that the groaning is focused on the Spirit's work of intercession according to the will of God.

C.S. Lewis once wrote, "If we find ourselves with a desire that nothing in this world can satisfy, the most probable explanation is that we were made for another world."[63] This is his famous 'argument from desire'. As we long for growth, progress, and advancement, we must come to grips with the fact that this world will never be able to satisfy those longings.

And, I believe, the Bible presents a similar argument of desire here in Romans 8. You see the groaning that we experience is ultimately that desire within us longing for another world. It is indeed the Spirit that is groaning for this new world. As we ourselves groan of the future, all of creation is looking forward to the resurrection. The reason the Spirit groans for the resurrection is because He is the Spirit of resurrection (Romans 8:11).

Once again N.T. Wright says,

> *The Spirit who brooded over the waters of chaos, the Spirit who indwelt Jesus so richly that He became known as the Spirit of Jesus: this Spirit, already present within Jesus's followers as the first fruits, the down payment, the guarantee of what is to come, is not only the beginning of the future life, even in the present time, but also the energizing power through which the final transformation will take place.*[64]

---

[63] C.S. Lewis, *Mere Christianity* (Macmillan, 1977).
[64] N.T. Wright, *Surprised by Hope: Rethinking Heaven, The Resurrection, and the Mission of the Church* (New York: Harper-Collins,

The Spirit of God groans within us now, longing for the day of resurrection. For He knows that day is coming. We must be convinced as well.

Jesus' Resurrection: The Turning Point in History

All of this talk about the resurrection can be quite odd, even for orthodox Christians. The strange belief of corpses coming back to life sounds like a horror movie. But bodily resurrection is the core Christian truth that distinctively makes Christianity stand apart from other systems of beliefs. This is because the resurrection of Jesus provides the shape and meaning to our hope.[65] The resurrection of Jesus is the means by which you and I have a living hope (1 Peter 1:3-4). The resurrection is the demonstration of God's power (Ephesians 1:20). Jesus' resurrection validates that our sins are forgiven (1 Corinthians 15:12-19). His resurrection is the grounds for our resurrection (2 Corinthians 4:14-5:10).

One important claim that the resurrection makes is stated in Romans 1:4. There the Apostle writes that Jesus "was appointed to be the powerful Son of God according to the Spirit of holiness by the resurrection of the dead." Now this doesn't mean that Jesus wasn't the Son of God prior to the resurrection. Rather the resurrection declares that this had always been the case.[66] Jesus was given a *new status* in the universe. He is indeed the Messiah, the rightful Lord. The Risen Lord now holds the keys of death and Hades (Revelation 1:17-18).

The truth claim that Jesus physically walked out of the tomb on a Sunday morning with a new body ought to encourage us. Because He was raised, death no longer has dominion. If we were to trace Paul's argument in 1 Corinthians 15, we would discover that our victory over death is solely

---

2008), 163.

[65] N.T. Wright, *Surprised by Hope*, 148

[66] Wright, *The Resurrection of the Son of God* (Minneapolis: Fortress Press, 2033), 733.

based on Christ's victory over death. This is a promise that although we will die, there is life *after* life after death.[67] Christ arose, Christ arose, hallelujah, Christ arose!

Resurrection and New Creation

The late John Lennon's famous song, "Imagine", was released in 1971. In the midst of a war-torn world Lennon's words sought to inspire the imagination. He imagined a world without countries, religion, and possessions. In the chorus we hear:

> *Imagine all the people, living life in peace…I hope someday you will join us, and the world will be as one.*

I submit that Lennon was right to a certain extent. We should imagine a world that lives in peace, a world existing as one. The world and her citizens are attempting to see this rule of peace. I write this section in the midst of a pandemic, an economic crisis, and civil unrest. As I watch the news and scroll through social media, there is an apparent desire for peace.

However, Lennon's anti-religion and anti-capitalist utopia was simply a dream. The world is too broken for this type of reality. Lennon's imagined world doesn't provide a solution to the world's problems. As broken humans, we are looking for true justice.

The injustice in the world is evidence that something is messed up. The fact of the matter is the injustices in this world are a result of our individual rebellion and the power of Sin that rules over a fallen humanity. Yet Scripture reveals that this present evil age is moving towards the *telos* where God's retributive and restorative justice is once and for all revealed. Therefore, the New Testament envisions a world in which peace, justice, and grace reigns. This is the world of the New Creation.

---

[67] Wright, *Surprised by Hope*, 148-149.

This is an eschatological reality where God's justice brings about shalom through the marriage of Heaven and Earth. The ungodly, Death, Hades, the Dragon are cast into the lake of fire and the resurrected saints enter into God's peaceable kingdom. The punishment of the ungodly, the resurrection of the dead, and the establishment of the New Creation are God's final acts of retributive and restorative justice.

The revelation of God's restorative justice is located in the resurrection. The resurrection then is God's final verdict of those who have faith in Jesus, whereby He vindicates them by triumphing over death itself. Death is therefore judged and God's justice is revealed. Michael Bird states, "Those who denied justice and inflicted injustices receive justice at the end. God's people rejoice, the nations worship God, and the entire universe gives God glory."[68]

In the present, we as the Church anticipate this eschatological reality and live as a signpost of God's coming justice. Bird again argues,

> *The church is meant to be the billboard for the world to come…The life of the church is to hint at what the world would look like in a redeemed state: righteousness flowing like a river, lions lying down with lambs, swords beaten into plowshares, and grace and mercy mingling together. We can work for justice in this world as part of our preparations for the next world.*[69]

Practically, as the Church we have experienced the justice of God in the person of Jesus. As a result, we are called to live out God's justice in this world as a preview for the next. We are the signpost of the coming Kingdom. The way in which God's justice impacts our individual lives through the death of Jesus ought to shape the way we live in this

---

[68] Michael Bird, *Evangelical Theology: A Biblical and Systematic Theology* (Grand Rapids: Zondervan, 2013), 307.
[69] Bird, *Evangelical Theology*, 308.

world now in light of God's eschatological justice.

Whether this involves calling those who commit injustice in this world to repent or treating our neighbor the way we want to be treated, God's justice as revealed in the person of Jesus is displayed through the Church.

Imagine a world like this; where justice and righteousness rules! The New Creation is the marriage of heaven and earth, a world without tears, fears, and pain. This world is so much better than Lennon's world. This coming New Creation is guaranteed through the resurrection of Jesus. We should imagine this world and seek to live in the present, as it will be in the future.[70]

Union with Christ and the Resurrection

D.A. Carson has said, "I'm not suffering from anything that a good resurrection can't fix."[71] And One Day resurrection will fix everything! As humans we have a future orientation. We desire a world of hope. Most importantly, we need this new world because our identity in Christ points beyond the present to the not yet. Even my daughter knows that when I leave to go to work, I will return. As she asks, "Where are you going?" she knows that I'll be back. She knows that I'm going somewhere but there is anticipation for my return. We know where we are going and we anticipate that day when Jesus returns, to make all things right. So, let's long for the future, believing that it will impact our present life now. The resurrection will give way to this new world.

The resurrection directs our cruciform identity. We must be reminded in the trials of life, the present isn't all there is. We are resurrected people, longing for resurrection (Ephesians 2:4-7). This is who we are—people longing for the future. And this future is bending towards Jesus. Since He was raised from the dead, one day we will join Him as

---

[70] Wright, *Evil and the Justice of God*, 128.
[71] https://www.desiringgod.org/articles/do-not-fear-growing-old-with-him

we sing over death the words of Paul, "Death where is your victory?" One day, death itself will die. That will be a good day. This resurrected New Creational future shape our identity. Our future goal is shaped like Jesus and all the glory goes to Jesus. As Dr. Moore writes, "Jesus Christ embodies the meaning of life, the goal of history, and the pattern of the future."[72] And we are "in Him."

---

[72] https://www.christianitytoday.com/ct/2012/february/jesus-afterlife.html

CHAPTER FIVE

Cruciform Identity and the Sovereignty of God

William Cowper is known for his powerful hymns such as *There is a Fountain Filled with Blood*. But his hymn, *God Moves in a Mysterious Way*, is honestly my favorite. The hymn paints a picture of God's loving sovereignty and demonstrates the mysterious acts of God behind human suffering. In the hymn he states,

> *Judge not the Lord by feeble sense, but trust Him for His grace; behind a frowning providence, He hides a smiling face.*[73]

John Piper, in a lecture on Cowper, discusses the deep depression of the hymn writer from the 18th century.[74] Much like Piper, I am drawn to William because I myself struggle with despair at times while believing in the sovereignty of God. You see, often times we do judge the Lord by feeble senses. We interpret our lives through our subjective experience. We grow weary because of our circumstances and at times lose faith. Yet what seems like a frowning providence, is actually the smiling face of our Father.

---

[73] https://www.challies.com/articles/hymn-stories-god-moves-in-a-mysterious-way/

[74] https://www.desiringgod.org/messages/insanity-and-spiritual-songs-in-the-soul-of-a-saint

Suffering, Pain, and Heartache

If you're like me, you've probably asked the question: *why am I suffering?* I recall the moment when I voiced this question to God. I was standing beside my daughter's hospital bed, looking at my one-month-old baby struggling for air. We had been in the hospital for four days at that point. We were tired and without answers. I felt helpless and hopeless. I had just been called to serve as pastor of a local church a month before Sophia went into the hospital. To complicate the suffering, I had just received my first "death call" as a pastor. It seemed like the world was falling apart. Why would God allow such suffering? I asked God, "Why are you doing this? Do you love me and my family?"

We've all been there in that moment when it seems as if God isn't there. His presence is absent. We have all experienced that "dark night of the soul" moment. Even the Psalmist cries out, "Why are you down cast, my soul?" (Psalm 42:5) Can you relate?

Suffering comes in many forms. It can be physical, emotional, and even spiritual. One particular form of suffering is mental. For the past several years I have been advocating for those struggling with mental health disorders. There seems to be a mental health crisis in our culture. And yet often times the Church doesn't know how to speak directly to the issue. We paint on our "happy face" to go to church and sit in our pews while we die inside.

I want you to know, if you struggle with mental health related issues you are not alone. Even the Apostle himself battled depression. Paul says in 2 Corinthians 1:8 that he "despaired of life itself." But here is hope, humanly speaking. This same Apostle wrote Romans 8:28-31. Suffering is a part of the Christian experience that shapes us for the future glory. And my brother and sister, please know, that glory is coming. This glory is not some pie-in-the-sky type of thing; rather it is tangible and real. It is resurrection and New Creation.

Cruciform Identity and the Sovereignty of God

But we still have to acknowledge our present pain. For this reason, Paul launches into one of the most encouraging paragraphs in all of his writings. What we see in Romans 8:28-30 is that God uses the suffering (all things) for good in our lives. Paul is giving us a divine perspective from eternity past, to the present, and then to eternity future.

All Things Work Together

We know that all things work together for the good of those who love God, who are called according to his purpose. Romans 8:28

Growing up, I attended a Vacation Bible School at the local Presbyterian church. I don't remember much from that VBS other than making sand art jars and Romans 8:28. Even though at the time I was more fascinated with the colorful sand art, Romans 8:28 reminds me of the colors of life coming together to make something beautiful.

What is missed often times is that the *all things* isn't referring just to the good things of life. In the context it appears that the all things entail suffering, trials, and hardship. But the passage says that *all things work together,* meaning that nothing is outside the control of God's providence. The specific Greek word for work together is *sunergei,* where we get our English word synergy. The seemly random pieces of our lives cooperate and gel together by the Sovereign hand of God. It's implied from the context that God is the One *working all things together.* Nothing takes God by surprise; nothing is beyond His sovereign activity.

While we may not fully understand it, we must trust the sovereignty of God. As I'm writing this chapter I'm sitting on my front porch. It's a wonderful place to write, think, and pray. Towards the West, the sun is beginning to set behind the trees and will pass beyond the horizon. This divine act of God paints a beautiful East Texas sky. From my front porch everything looks nice. But I'm writing this chapter in the midst of the 2020 COVID-19 pandemic, just having recovered from the virus myself. I am quarantined. All the while, many lives I know personally are being altered because of this present pandemic. I find myself reminded once again that our sovereign God is working everything together, even though I don't fully understand it.

The Purpose of God's Sovereignty

But why does God work all things together? He does it *for good*. We must understand that this is referring to God's good, not ours. We must trust that God's good is better than ours. We can only see a few things happening in our lives but God knows all things. But notice the Bible doesn't say that all things are good. Many things that take place in our lives aren't necessarily good. Suffering, trials, pain, and heartache hurt. However, Spurgeon said, "Trials cut the ropes which fasten our souls to earthly things."[75]

We need to understand that God uses the trials and suffering for our good. "Good" here is probably a reference to our salvation and eternal purpose of life. We may not understand "the how or the why" but we can trust the Who is behind all things in our lives.

I want you to note that this promise is applied to, first of all, "those who love God." This is an interesting way of putting it. Paul is highlighting our response to God's work in our lives. We love God for what He has done for us. Secondly, it says, "Those called according to His purpose." This is the flip side of salvation. God has called us to his purpose, the eternal purpose of mercy. This one verse is pregnant with truth! You do not live at the hands of fate or random chance. Rather, we have a sovereign God guiding each step and circumstance. I know that God is working all things out because I love Him and He has called me to Himself.

---

[75] https://www.ccel.org/ccel/spurgeon/sermons52.xxvi.html

Have you ever seen a beautiful mosaic? If you stand too close to it all you see is random shapes and colors. You might see different images and pictures. It looks like chaos. But as you move back to see the whole picture, those random images form one complete piece of art. Our lives are like a mosaic. Most of the time we only see the random shapes. Up close, things look like a mess but from a divine perspective it is a beautiful masterpiece. This is the truth of this verse.

We see the "all things" as random chaos. But in God's plan He is working it all out for His glory and our ultimate good. This is the God who reigns in glory! The late Baptist preacher Adrian Rogers once said, "If there were not a God in glory, there would not be the promise of Romans 8:28 in the Bible."[76]

Why Do All Things Work Together?

Yet the question is *why* do all things work together for good? The passage presents four reasons why all things work together for good. First, the Bible says that *God has loved and chosen us before time to look like Jesus*. It says that *"those he foreknew, He predestined to be conformed into the image of Jesus."*

Now, I want to be clear: the language of foreknowledge and predestination are sticky theological terms. These words have been debated since the original writing. But I do want you to understand that these realities are applied to those who believe in Christ. You see the passage makes clear that these realities are true for believers.

The word of "foreknew" carries the idea of God's eternal action of loving us before time while "predestined" is God's eternal action of choosing of us before time. Again, these terms are loaded and space does not permit an in-depth discussion. But these truths should bring us comfort!

---

[76] From a seminar given by Adrian Rogers: https://billygraham.org/story/do-all-things-work-together-for-good/

Paul says in Ephesians 1:3-6 that God chose us "in Christ" (very important to understand that election, calling, salvation, perseverance are in Christ). Election, predestination, and other weighty theological realities are only applied to believers because they are *in Christ* by faith. Faith is our personal response to Christ's work. You see God has loved us before time and has chosen us to look like Jesus.[77] Think about this: before you were born, God loved you and had a plan for your life. By faith, His plan becomes our purpose. That's the intention of the passage. This very truth provides us clarity in understanding our identity and purpose.

But we shouldn't miss the goal of God's predestining work, namely our conformity into the image of Jesus. God's goal is to make us look like Jesus, act like Jesus, and love like Jesus. Here is where we find *"what the working of all things together looks like."* It looks like personal conformity into the image of Christ. He takes everything in your life and uses it to make you look like Jesus. The aim of all of this is glory, specifically giving glory of King Jesus. This Biblical truth parallels many of the great confessions of the faith. Election is a means of sanctification.

This sanctifying truth is echoed in the 1833 Baptist Confession:

> *We believe that Election is the eternal purpose of God, according to which he graciously regenerates, sanctifies, and saves sinners; that being perfectly consistent with the free agency of man, it comprehends all the means in connection with the end…*[78]

Why do all things work out for the good? It's simple: God has loved us and has chosen us to look like Jesus. By

---

[77] It's important to note that here in Romans 8:28-30 that the language of *foreknowledge and predestination* are primarily about sanctification.

[78] 1833 New Hampshire Baptist Confession, which is the basis for the Baptist Faith and Message 2000.

faith, this amazing reality becomes ours. This was God's action before time. God had a plan for your life before you even existed.

The second reason all things work together for good is because *God has summoned us into a relationship with Himself.* He has called to us to Himself. This is referring to a personal summons into a relationship. God desires that you and I know Him personally. Since God chooses us, He summons us into a loving relationship with Him. We are invited to respond by faith to God's call. We are called to be His. This is referring to God's action in time. Simply put, this is divine intentionality!

The third reason for all things working together for good is referring to another action of God in time. *God has declared us in right standing through the death of Jesus.* We are justified, which means we are declared in right standing before God. This is on the basis of Christ's work. Implied in this truth, is our responsibility of personal belief. God acts to call us through the gospel and we respond by trusting His Son's atoning work. We must not neglect human responsibility. While this is true, the emphasis of the passage is the Divine action of God. After loving us before time, choosing us in time, and summoning us into a relationship, He then declares us right through the work of Jesus (Romans 5:1).

The last reason why all things work together for good is because *God has already decided to glorify us in the future.* As discussed in the last chapter, we will one day be glorified in the resurrection. If you were to break down the Greek text, you'd notice that the verbs are paralleled together. The verbs are in the aorist tense (indicating an action that took place in the past).[79] Basically, Paul describes this event with certainty from a divine perspective. The decision to glorify those who have been justified has already been made. God can speak this way if he loved us before time, chose us in time, summoned us into a relationship, and declared us in

---

[79] http://www.ntgreek.net/lesson22.htm

right standing through the work of Christ. If He has already accomplished these actions for us, it is a promise that He will glorify us in the future. It is certain! God's providential acts before time, provide assurance, despite our problems in time.

Suffering and the Sovereignty of God

Suffering is tough. The trials of life can blindside us and, in some cases, destroy our faith. As a pastor there have been many occasions, I've entered a counseling session and be confronted by the question, "Why is God…?" Whether it is an unexpected death of a loved one or an unexpected diagnosis, the question "why" is at the forefront of our minds. I'm convinced we all became theologians when suffering hits us.

Before we end this chapter, we must note this important truth. The passage does not say that God is the author of your suffering. Questions such as "Does God ordain suffering?" or "Does He just allow suffering to happen?" really isn't the point of the passage. While we need to ask such questions and seek for answers, this isn't necessarily the point of the passage under consideration. We must allow the given Scripture to speak on its own without imposing our personal questions upon it. Sometimes our questions aren't specifically answered in every passage. Pastorally though, I sense it necessary to address this issue.

The issue of God's goodness and the problem of evil has dominated religious and philosophical conversation for centuries.[80] While rehearsing these arguments isn't necessary for our purpose in this book, I would encourage you to pick up John Piper and Justin Taylor edited a work entitled *Suffering and the Sovereignty of God*, which seeks to provide

---

[80] https://www.thegospelcoalition.org/essay/the-problem-of-evil/

Cruciform Identity and the Sovereignty of God

clarity on this very question.[81] However, I would like to address the issue in two ways.

First, while it may sound controversial, we must realize that our God is not distant from pain and suffering. In the incarnation, God took upon flesh in the person of Jesus. In the event of the cross, our good God experienced suffering in Christ. When God entered into our human experience in the person of Jesus, He Himself experienced the fullness of our suffering on the cross.

The Transcendent One became intimately familiar with our pain. Allow me to quote John Stott in full:

> *I could never myself believe in God, if it were not for the cross. The only God I believe in is the One Nietzsche ridiculed as 'God on the cross.' In the real world of pain, how could one worship a God who was immune to it? I have entered many Buddhist temples in different Asian countries and stood respectfully before the statue of the Buddha, his legs crossed, arms folded, eyes closed, the ghost of a smile playing round his mouth, a remote look on his face, detached from the agonies of the world. But each time after a while I have had to turn away. And in imagination I have turned instead to that lonely, twisted, tortured figure on the cross, nails through hands and feet, back lacerated, limbs wrenched, brow bleeding from thorn pricks, mouth dry and intolerably thirsty, plunged in Godforsaken darkness. That is the God for me! He laid aside his immunity to pain. He entered our world of flesh and blood, tears and death. He suffered for us.*[82]

While we may not fully understand this and while we should not deny the classical doctrine of the Trinity, in some way our God in His infinite wisdom condescended to experience our own suffering. When our Lord Jesus cried out *"My God, my God why have you forsaken me"* the weight of our

---

[81] John Piper and Justin Taylor, *Suffering and the Sovereignty of God* (Wheaton: Crossway, 2006).
[82] John Stott, *The Cross of Christ*, 335-336.

sin and the brokenness of the world veiled the face of the Father. In this moment the Lord of Glory, God the Son incarnate drank our agony and pain; it was God in our nature forsaken by God.[83] As Spurgeon once said,

> *At one tremendous draught of love, He drank damnation dry for all his people. He drank it all, he endured all, he suffered all; so that now forever there are no flames of hell for them, no racks of torment; they have no eternal woes; Christ hath suffered all they ought to have suffered, and they must, they shall go free.*[84]

God's suffering love shouldn't cause us to doubt His unchangeably.[85] Yet what we see in the cross is a God in complete control, a God who willingly takes upon Himself the suffering of humanity. For the believer, when suffering strikes, you must know that God is intimately present with you. He has not removed Himself from your pain. He is there. As Stott says, "The cross of Christ is the proof of God's solidary love, that is, of His personal, loving solidarity with us in our pain."[86]

The second way we should understand the problem of evil as it relates to God is knowing that God will ultimately rid the world of suffering. As has been the repeated theme throughout the last few chapters, our hope is indeed the resurrection. Through the resurrection and into the New Creation our God will rectify the problem of evil. The completely remedy for suffering is ultimately eschatological. The

---

[83] Murray, *Redemption Accomplished and Applied* (Grand Rapids: Eerdmans, 1955), 77.

[84] Charles Spurgeon, *The New Park Street Pulpit Sermons, Vol. III* (London: Passmore & Alabaster, 1855), 155. Sermon No. 126; Titled: Justification by Grace; Delivered on Sabbath Morning, April 5th, 1857.

[85] John Frame, *The Doctrine of God, A Theology of Lordship* (New Jersey: P&R Publishing, 202), 616.

[86] Stott, *The Cross of Christ*, 329.

Cruciform Identity and the Sovereignty of God

resurrection is God's "yes" to life and restoration over the "no" of suffering and death.

So, whether God is the primary cause for suffering or not doesn't change the fact that God Himself is still in control. The New Testament does indeed suggest that God uses suffering in ways to shape us (1 Peter 1:6-9). Yet there is a balance in seeing that God is indeed the author of the story (including our individuals lives) but is not the author of evil.[87]

Therefore, we must respond to suffering and evil in this world with wisdom, knowing that nothing is outside of His sovereignty. The promise of Romans 8:28-30 is that God providentially works all things together to His desired end. We could say that God providentially arranges each specific situation and sovereignly, in tandem with our free choices, carries us along to the ultimate good by the Spirit.[88] This is all a matter of faith.

Union with Christ and the Sovereignty of God

The sovereignty of God must be the pillow on which we lay our heads as believers. As we trust in God's good plan, we rest knowing He has it understand control. Even when our world is spinning upside down, our God is right side up. William Cowper, in that beautiful hymn, concludes,

> *His purposes will ripen fast, Unfolding every hour; The bud may have a bitter taste, But sweet will be the flower.*

While much of life may have a bitter taste, we can trust that one day, the flower will bloom. Romans 8:28-30 is a means of encouragement to those who are in Christ. Your life from beginning to end is under the providence of almighty God. He is sovereign. He is good. So, you can trust that He is working all things together for good. The truth

---

[87] Frame, *The Doctrine of God*, 181.
[88] Frame, *The Doctrine of God*, 286.

should stir our minds and comfort our hearts. The sovereignty of God provides a stable ground for our cruciform identity. God has all things in His hands and nothing will escape His eye. What are you experiencing right now that is causing you to doubt God's plan? The Bible tells us that "in Christ" He is working all things for good.

CHAPTER SIX

Cruciform Identity and Eternity Security

Among my conversations with Christians, there are two topics that always come up: *suffering and sin*. These two realities in our lives cause many issues. The truth is, we all suffer and we all sin. But for many Christians, the questions about suffering and sin can usually be boiled down into two main questions:

First, when I suffer does God even love me?
Second, when I sin am I even saved?

We don't have an adequate framework for understanding suffering and sin because our experiences and emotions become our interpretive grid. When I suffer, I tend to respond emotionally from my pain. When I sin, I respond out of my shame. So, attempting to answer these questions about sin and suffering based on emotion can lead to confusing and hurtful answers. But all of this boils down to the issue of security. Am I truly safe? The truth is we all desire security.

Many of us have been victims of broken relationships due to suffering and sin, causing us to have trust issues. We fear instability and insecurity. Quite frankly, often times we apply these experiences to God. But Romans 8:31-39 has the answer to the question:

> *In the midst of the suffering and sin, am I truly safe or has God separated Himself from me?*

The Grace of God and the God of Grace

As we have moved through Romans 8, exploring its theology, we've sought to understand our union with Christ and its impact upon our identity. However, we must remind ourselves that we are "already but not yet" people. We are still broken in a broken world.

As a result, Romans 8 is a much-needed balm of grace for our wounds. The first thirty verses of Romans 8 have set forth the *adequacy of the grace of God* that deals with the issues of life. This grace is seen in justification, the giving of the Spirit, and the hope of resurrection. But we can't miss what happens between verse 30 and 31 in this wonderful Biblical chapter. Paul transitions from the grace of God to the God of grace as our sole assurance in the Christian life. Packer says, "His [Paul's] theme shifts slightly and becomes the *adequacy of the God of grace*."[89] Romans 8:31-39 is Paul's experiential and theological announcement that God—who is Father, Son, and Spirit—is the establishment of our entire existence.

No One is Able to Prevail Against You Because of God's Love

Paul states a true and powerful reality: *Since God has worked on our behalf, no one can be against us*. The idea is to prevail against us either by actions or by words. God is for us, meaning he has acted on our behalf. The question is *how is God for us?* First and foremost, God has provided Jesus and will give us all things to live for Him. Echoing back to

---

[89] Packer, *Knowing God* (Downers Grove: IVP, 1993), 258.

Romans 8:1, God has provided all that we need in order to be saved and He continues to provide for us in order to be sanctified. If God has given all things in His Son, how much more will He give us all things for our relationship with Him?

Since God is for you, *no one can accuse you because God has justified you.* Paul says that no one can accuse you or bring a charge against you. Practically speaking, no one can say, "This person isn't a Christian!" The reason why is because God has already justified you, meaning He has declared you righteous based upon the work of Christ. I want you to see the picture. You've already been to the courtroom of God and since God doesn't accuse you, no one can. This justification is final and eternal. To say it this way: our justification is our present verdict in anticipation of the final judgment.[90] Wright in his book *Justification* states,

> *The present verdict gives the assurance that the future verdict will match it; the Spirit gives the power through which that future verdict, when given, will be seen to be in accordance with the life that the believer has then lived.*[91]

It never fails that when a Christian mess up, there is always someone there to accuse them. There is always that person saying, "Well they can't be a Christian!" To compound that, when suffering enters our lives, we often hear the voice of our greatest enemy saying, "God doesn't love you and never has." What the Bible says is that since God has already worked in our lives to free us from condemnation, there is absolutely no one who can accuse us. If you are in Christ the present verdict of "justified" looks forward to the final announcement when we stand before Christ.

---

[90] Wright, *Justification: God's Plan and Paul's Vision* (Downers Grove: IVP, 2009), 239.
[91] Wright, *Justification*, 251.

But Paul continues by saying that *no one can condemn you since Christ has acted on your behalf.* This means that no one can pronounce a sentence of "guilty" upon you! No one can condemn you because Christ has acted on your behalf.

The Bible makes it clear why this is possible. Notice His actions:

- First: Jesus Died for Your Sin (Romans 3:21-26 – Sacrifice)
- Second: He is Raised from the Dead (Romans 4:25 – Messiah)
- Third: He Reigns at God's Right Hand (Romans 1:1-2 – Kingly Son of God)
- Fourth: Christ Intercedes for us (He is our Great High Priest)

I want you to understand this: because of God's love, in providing Christ for you and justifying you, no one can prevail against you in word or deed. No one can accuse you and no one can condemn you. By this I mean *no one*—Satan cannot condemn you. Your sin cannot condemn you. Your past cannot condemn you. You cannot condemn you! Because of Christ, you are in Him and you are free. The One Being in the universe that had every right to bring condemnation chooses not to because His Son was condemned in your place.

So how do you fight against the accusations of others? I believe when an accusation is made, you claim it and look to Jesus. When Satan says, "God doesn't love you!" You respond with "I don't deserve His love but He gives it anyway!" When your sin seeks to condemn, you argue, "Yes, I am a sinner, but Christ! Yes, I am guilty, but Christ. Yes, I deserve judgment, but Christ!" When that one person says, "You can't be a Christian" declare, "I am not perfect but I have a Perfect Savior!"

Cruciform Identity and Eternal Security

Your identity does not come from your personal achievements or failures. Nor does your identity come from words of praise or criticism. But if we're honest we are prone to seek out the approval of others. When reject flow from the lips of family members and friends their words seem to pierce our hearts. This is why the Bible says that our identity in Christ secures us. While criticism, accusations, or rejection may come there is nothing that can separate from God in Christ.

Absolutely Nothing is Able to Separate You from God's Love

The Apostle Paul continues by saying that *no amount of external opposition can separate you from God's love.* The Apostle quotes Psalm 44:22, which proves that God's people have always experienced suffering. The people of God have already and will continue to experience opposition in this life. But the truth is no amount of human suffering will be able to remove you from God's love. Listen to this: that 'thing' that is causing you suffering can never separate you from God.

The reason why, is because the people of God *are triumphant over these things, and absolutely nothing can separate us.* The Bible says we are "more than conquerors" through Jesus. Specifically, we are triumphant over the things that harm us and those things that attempt to separate us from God because of Jesus. Consider the list of items that Paul names:

- Death and the Problems of Life
- Spiritual Powers
- Present or Future Circumstances
- Natural or Supernatural Forces
- Anything in Heaven or Hell
- Anything else in Creation

Basically, Paul is saying that there is not one thing in this life or the life to come that will ever be able to remove us from God's love. Sin can't do it. Suffering can't do it. Not even death itself can separate us from God's love in Christ.

Eternal Security: The Keeping Power of God

Despite the trials, circumstances, and sufferings in this life, nothing is able to separate you from God's love. His love is stronger than those things that attempt to separate us from him. This is the truth of eternal security. Because of God's love for you in Christ, you are eternally saved. Here is the argument: The Father loves His Son eternally. This means there will never be a moment when the Father will stop loving the Son.

If you are in Christ, you are loved by the Father with the same love that He has for His Son. This means there will never be a moment when the Father will stop loving you. Because, if the Father stopped loving you, it would mean He stopped loving His own Son. This means there is nothing that will ever prevent the Father from loving you, if you are in Christ! In your suffering, God has not forsaken you. In your sin, God has not stopped loving you. His desire for you is to grow into the image of Jesus.

The New Testament provides a clear picture of our eternal security. In John's Gospel we hear Jesus's words, "No one will snatch them out of my hand" (John 10:28). Jude writes, "Now to Him who is able to protect you from stumbling…" (Jude 24). Once again Paul writes, "He who started a good work in you will carry it on to completion until the day of Christ Jesus" (Philippians 1:6).
Bruce Demarest provides a beautiful summary of the doctrine of eternal security:

> *Our comfort and hope derives from the certainty that the Father in all His perfections will not permit His children to be lost, that the Son will not allow His sheep to be snatched from His hands, and that the Holy Spirit infallibly seals the saints unto the day*

> *of consummated redemption. In the final analysis, the hope of true believers resides not in our feeble hold of God but in His powerful grasp of us.*[92]

God's love for His Son is never-ending and because you are in Christ, you can never experience a moment in which God will ever stop loving you. The Father will never abandon you because the Son has already experienced true abandonment in your place. When you feel forsaken, know that it is just a feeling and not a reality. His love for you is not predicated on your performance but on Christ's work, which was on your behalf. It is in this truth that we find hope. There is nothing that can separate us from His love.

Union with Christ and Eternal Security

You see our union with Christ by faith provides us eternal security. You and I are eternally protected because of Christ's saving power, the Spirit's sealing power, and the Father's keeping power. Our eternal security undergirds our cruciform identity. Despite suffering and sin, you are safe in Christ. Your identity, your life, and your future are wrapped up in Jesus.

Many churches have adopted the Heidelberg Catechism, which was written in 1563. Like all catechisms, it provides a series of questions and answers that establish Christian doctrine. Though the Heidelberg Catechism is not part of my Christian tradition, I find the first question and answer a powerful testimony to the beauty of the gospel. Listen to these words:

Question. *What is your only comfort in life and death?*

Answer. *That I am not my own, but belong with body and soul, both*

---

[92] Bruce Demarest, *The Cross and Salvation: The Doctrine of Salvation*, Foundations of Evangelical Theology (Wheaton: Crossway, 1997), 460.

in life and in death, to my faithful Savior Jesus Christ. He has fully paid for all my sins with His precious blood, and has set me free from all the power of the devil. He also preserves me in such a way that without the will of my heavenly Father not a hair can fall from my head; indeed, all things must work together for my salvation. Therefore, by His Holy Spirit He also assures me of eternal life and makes me heartily willing and ready from now on to live for Him.[93]

---

[93] https://students.wts.edu/resources/creeds/heidelberg.html

CHAPTER SEVEN

The Truth of Our Cruciform Identity

In his book, *Knowing God*, J.I. Packer writes,

Do I, as a Christian, understand myself? Do I know my own real identity? My own real destiny? I am a child of God. God is my Father; heaven is my home; every day is one day nearer. My Savior is my brother; every Christian is my brother too…This is the Christian's secret of a Christian life, and of a God-honoring life, and these are the aspects of the situation that really matter.[94]

I propose that Romans 8 opens the door for this God-honoring life. This chapter is the Mount Everest of Scripture! It presents the beautiful picture of our identity in Christ. We are not condemned, we possess the life-giving Spirit, we are resurrection bound, and we are secure for all of eternity. However, there is one thing that often prevents us from living this truth out: sin. Our individual sin derails our Christian walk and our identity. It hinders. It hurts. It halts. This brings us back to the very issue we discussed in chapter 1. Our sin creates a crisis of identity.

Yet if your desire is to pursue Christ and experience His presence, we must understand how we can kill the sin within us. I'm convinced it comes down the reality that we've been

---

[94] J.I. Packer, *Knowing God*, 228.

discussing—understanding our identity in Christ and His power within us.

Located within the same context of Romans 8 is the section of Romans 6:1-14. It is here where the Apostle Paul sets forth the theological implications of the Christian life regarding sin. What we'll see is that our union with Christ becomes the basis for our war against sin.

The Truth of Our Cruciform Identity

In Romans 6 the Apostle Paul introduces an idea from Romans 5. If the grace of God abounded when people sinned, they why don't we just continue to live in our sin in order that grace can abound all the more? Should we continue to live in our old way of life so that God can pour out more grace to us? Unfortunately, many people believe this way. Although as good Christians we would never outright say it, sometimes we can fall into the thought process of, *"Oh. I'm a Christian, I'm forgiven, so I can live the way I want to live and God will forgive me no matter what!"* The good news is that God does forgive us when we sin. But the temptation for many believers is to think that grace somehow provides a license to sin. The Bible makes it clear that grace is not a license to sin but grace provides us liberty not to sin.

The Bible claims that as believers, we have actually died to sin. But seriously, what does that even mean? As we examine our lives, we realize that we *still sin*. We trip, fall, and stumble into the sin that we have repented of in the past. So why does the Bible say we have *died to sin*? It's important to understand what it doesn't mean. First it doesn't mean that we won't be tempted by sin. Also, it doesn't mean that we won't sin. Finally, it doesn't mean that we are perfect.

Rather it means that we've been delivered from the absolute tyranny of sin, from the state in which sin holds us captive, the state in which we all lived before we were saved—habitual sinning reveals sin's tyranny, a tyranny from which the believer has been freed.[95] The very thing that controlled us (the power of sin) has now lost its power! The Point: How can we continue to live in sin, if we have died to sin?

But how have we died to sin? Paul states that we have been *baptized into Christ*, which means we were baptized into His death. The temptation is to read baptism as water baptism. But Paul isn't specifically referring to our physical baptism at this point. Rather *baptism into Christ* is a spiritual baptism by faith. This is another way Paul can describe your salvation experience. In the moment you placed your faith in Christ, you were baptized into Christ.

Theology of Union with Christ

Once again, we encounter the profound idea of union with Christ in the phrase *baptized into Christ*. In the passage of Romans 6:1-14 Paul uses the phrases *"united with Christ", "crucified with Him", "died with Christ", and "in Christ Jesus."* All of these phrases speak of the same spiritual reality. As we've explored throughout this book, our union with Christ is a real and spiritual experience. We are in a real and living union with Christ and currently participating in the benefits of His death and resurrection. It's imperative for us to understand that for Paul this is not metaphorical. It is nonetheless real and spiritual. As we've said, this is our crucified identity.

But let's take some time to really develop this idea of union with Christ. In his work, *Paul and Union with Christ*, Constantine Campbell identities the concept of union with Christ is best understood in four primary terms: union, participation, identification, and incorporation.[96] What this means is that the phrases *"in Christ", "through Christ," "with Christ"*, and similar usages in the Paul's writings convey a specific nuanced meaning.

---

[95] Moo, *Epistle to the Romans*, 413.
[96] Constantine Campbell, *Paul and Union with Christ: An Exegetical and Theology study* (Grand Rapids: Zondervan, 2021).

Let me illustrate. If I say to a friend, *I am with you*, the natural question is, *what do you mean with me?* The idea of being with you could mean, *I am identifying with you* or even *I am physically present with you.* The phrase 'with you' has a specific meaning once we understand it in context. The same principle applies to interpreting the phrase *with Christ* or *in Christ*.

Union

The phrase *in Christ* can obviously convey the idea of *union*. This union idea describes the mutual indwelling of Christ in the believer and the believer in Christ.[97] This idea many be hard to grasp, however, the idea of a "spiritual union" helps to clarify this reality. Using the word spiritual union conveys the believer's bond with Christ by His Spirit.[98] The use of spiritual doesn't mean it isn't *real*, rather, it is beyond our mere human comprehension. Some have suggested the idea of "mystical union."[99] The reality of the believer's mystical union with Christ doesn't mean that we somehow merge into Christ's divinity, rather the spiritual indwelling in the believer's heart makes us like Jesus.[100]

But let's be honest. Many Evangelical Christians may be slightly uncomfortable with the language of *mystical*. Unfortunately, the thoughts of weird paranormal activity as seen on goofy TV shows often come to the forefront of our minds when we hear the word *mystical*. However, the word mystical simple means mystery.[101] So when we use the word mystical it doesn't mean that somehow, we experience an ontological change (whoa big word), as in the believer now presently shares in Christ's divine nature. In no way do we

---

[97] Moo, The Epistle to the Romans, 413.
[98] Murray, *Redemption Accomplished and Applied* (Grand Rapids: Eerdmans, 1955), 176.
[99] Demarest, *The Cross and Salvation:* 324.
[100] Demarest, *The Cross and Salvation:* 324-325.
[101] Murray, *Redemption Accomplished and Applied*, 177.

become Jesus. Rather we are *becoming like Jesus* by our union with Him.

Rather, the idea means that we share in the saving and covenantal benefits of Christ.[102] For example the believer "in Christ" has been chosen, called, regenerated, justified, and one day will be glorified (Eph 1:3-14, Rom 8:28-30). However, we know that these saving benefits are not applied to us until we express personal faith in Christ. Our union with Christ is grounded in what Christ has done for us on the cross.[103]

Simple put: the spiritual mystery of our union with Christ is indeed a real and living reality for the believer. As John Murray states,

> *But it is union of an intensely spiritual character consonant with the nature and work of the Holy Spirit so that in a real way surpassing our power of analysis Christ dwells in His people and His people dwell in Him.*[104]

Let's provide some clarity to this idea of union. On June 15th, 2012, I said the words, "I Do" to a beautiful woman. We stood in front of witnesses, exchanged vows, and entered into a marriage union. In that moment everything I had became hers and everything she had, became mine. We became one. Our union with Christ is a marriage between Him and us. Everything He has is ours!

Participation

Second, the idea of "in Christ" is nuanced by the idea of *participation*. What does this mean? Basically, our spiritual union with Christ involves our participation in the gospel events of Christ's death, resurrection, exaltation, and

---

[102] Demarest *The Cross and Salvation:* 319
[103] Demarest, *The Cross and Salvation:* 321
[104] Murray, *Redemption Accomplished and Applied*, 177.

glorification (Col 3:1-4). Michael Gorman says that the narrative of Christ's life and death is the normative life-narrative of the believer.[105] This idea is that the believer is currently partaking in the gospel narrative of Jesus Himself. Theologically Christ's death becomes our death and His resurrection becomes our resurrection. When we trust in Christ, we become participants the gospel events of Christ.[106]

Now what does this mean practically? Paul uses this idea when he talks about the moral-ethical life of the believer. As Christ died and rose again, so we die and rise spiritually (2 Corinthians 5:14-15). While this may seem all theoretical at this point, let me show you the practical benefits of this idea. When we experience hardships and trials, the Bible says what we are share in the sufferings of Christ (2 Corinthians 1:3-11). You see the present sufferings and personal struggle against sin are an aspect of the participatory reality.[107] We are called to "die to self" and "live for God" (more will be said about this in the following chapters).

But here is the point: we are currently in a real spiritual yet practical way actively participating in the narrative of Christ (Ephesians 2:5-7).

Identification

The third idea of union with Christ can be understood in terms of *identification* with Christ. The idea behind this spiritual reality is that we are currently situated in the realm of Christ's Lordship, meaning that we belong to Christ and owe Him allegiance.[108] Our personal identification with

---

[105] Michael Gorman, *Cruciformity: Paul's Narrative Spirituality of the Cross* (Grand Rapids: Eerdmans, 2001), 44.

[106] Campbell, *Paul and Union with Christ: An Exegetical and Theology Study* (Grand Rapids: Zondervan, 2012), 377.

[107] Robert Tannehill, *Dying and Rising with Christ: A Study in Pauline Theology* (Eugene OR: Wipf and Stock, 2006), 81.

[108] Campbell, *Paul and Union with Christ,* 408.

Christ in Paul is revealed in baptism (Rom 6:1-5). Practically this means if you are a believer you have probably experienced baptism—fully immersed into water. If we are honest, the practice of baptism is kind of a weird ritual. For example, when I was 17 years old, I was baptized in a horse through (mind you I'm from East Texas). But when we understand that our visible baptism points to a spiritual reality, water baptism is less weird.

You see by faith you were spiritually baptized into Christ (you were saved) and your physical baptism symbolizes that real spiritual experience. We are baptized in water (a visible picture of death and resurrection) because we have already experienced a spiritual death and resurrection in Christ. Our physically baptism shows that we have been spiritual baptized into Christ's death and now raised to new life!

The Spirit brings about this identification with Christ. This is why Paul could say, "Your life is hidden with Christ in God...Christ who is your life..." (Col 3:3-4). This identification is closely tied to participation in that the believer is identified with Christ's death, resurrection, exaltation, and subsequent return.

Incorporation

Lastly union with Christ involves *incorporation* into Christ. This nuance shows the corporate dimensions of membership into Christ's body, the church.[109] Since we are united with Christ, we are incorporated into God's people. We are not just individuals doing our own individual thing in the world. Rather we are incorporated in a BIG family—God's family.

---

[109] Campbell, *Paul and Union with Christ*, 413.

Our Union is Our Freedom

We see the combination of these ideas come together in Romans 6:1-14. We are in Christ Jesus. We are united with Jesus. We participate with Him in His death and resurrection. We are identified with Him in baptism. And the result of this is our incorporation into His body, the church. His story becomes our story. If we really believe that Jesus actually died and was actually raised from the dead than our union with the real and living Christ is actually a real spiritual reality. This means you have now been transferred from one domain to a new domain. You and I were once in the domain of sin and death but now we are transferred into the domain of life and resurrection in Christ. When you trusted in Christ something happened to you—you were united to the exalted Lord!

In our personal lives we fight and war with the sin within and around us. But I'm convinced we need to grasp this truth. We are not just people struggling with sin, living in despair, waiting to die to go to heaven. That view of the Christian life is boring and miserable! We actually in a real and spiritual way have experienced a change in our identity because we are now united with Christ and participate in His life, death, and resurrection.

This is more than just theological pontification; it is profoundly practical. The transformation of your personal identity of being baptized into Christ shapes the way we view our lives, specifically regarding sin. As believers we still struggle with sin. As a pastor I've been asked many times "how do I overcome personal sin?"

I believe it comes down to this: *The way you view yourself in Christ fundamentally changes the way you live.* If we realize that in Christ, we are no longer a weak, miserable, and broken person. But in Christ we have died to sin because we have experienced a radical transformation. So, the practical question is *"will you die in sin or die to sin?"*

The Explanation of Our Cruciform Identity

Let's continue to look at how Paul explains this idea of "dead to sin" in Romans 6:5-8.

First: We have been united with Christ in the likeness of His death and resurrection. Our baptism into Christ means that we are united to His death and resurrection. This means are spiritually united with the crucified and Risen Christ. Our baptism into Christ means that we are spiritually participating in His death and resurrection, as we just discussed. Paul's emphasis is on the death and resurrection that has already taken place regarding our identity in Christ. Scripture teaches that one day we will all die and if we have trusted in Christ we will be raised from the dead. But the emphasis here in Romans 6 is on the NOW of our Christian experience.

Second: We know that our old self has already been crucified with Christ. Paul uses the word "body." In the passage the word doesn't refer to the physical body, rather, it is referring to the old you, the you that was once under the domain of sin. Listen to this truth! You see in the moment you placed your faith in Jesus, the old you was crucified. This means that the "former you"—*the you* who lived under the domain of sin and death—has died. The purpose is that the old self (the self under the control of sin) might be rendered powerless—meaning we aren't enslaved to sin anymore since we've been set free from sin.

Now understand I'm not intentionally being contrary but allow me to rehearse something at this point. As stated in chapter 1 I'm sure you've probably been taught—like I was—that a Christian has two natures, the sinful nature and the redeemed nature. While something like this may be true to a certain extent, it doesn't seem like Paul is actually saying this here in Romans 6. Rather he uses the language of *domain of existence or sphere of existence*. This means the old self, the self under the domain and control of sin, the self that was once enslaved to sin has indeed died; it does not control us, sin has no power over us because in Christ the old self in a real way has already been crucified.

Third: Since we have died with Christ we will live with Christ. Our death in Christ, which is our death to sin in the death of Christ, leads to our new life with Christ. Spiritually speaking we have already been raised to new life because of our union with Christ. As Tannehill says,

> *If the believer dies and rises with Christ, as Paul claims, Christ's death and resurrection are not merely events, which produce benefits for the believer but also are events in which the believer himself partakes. The believer's new life is based upon his personal participating in these saving events.*[110]

As we live day to day, our identity in Christ is being challenged. We see a culture that is diving deeper into depravity. Sin abounds all around us. So how does this important truth of dying to the old you change our identity? Hold onto this powerful truth: *In a real and spiritual way His death becomes our death and His resurrection our resurrection.* This is more than just a metaphor since the Spirit brings about this living union with Christ. Something very real takes place when the believer participates in the gospel events of Christ. This participatory reality of union with Christ transforms the way we live.

This means the things that once condemned you no longer have power of you. This is because in Christ our old self that was once under the control and domain of sin has already been crucified. Sin and death will one day be destroyed when Christ returns but *already,* we have experienced a death to our old self and a resurrection to new life. We must take this seriously. Believer, the "old you" that was under the domain of sin, has actually died in the death Christ and is now rendered powerless.

---

[110] See full discussion on Romans 6 in Tannehill, *Dying and Rising with Christ*, 77-84.

The Grounds of Our Cruciform Identity

As we continue to reflect upon Romans 6, Paul in verses 9-10 seeks to ground this truth in the work of Jesus Christ. Our dying and rising with Christ is grounded in the reality that Christ was died and was raised.

First the Bible claims that Christ is raised from the dead and He will never die again since death does not rule over Him. This is the gospel. Through His death and resurrection, Jesus is the One who has triumphed over death. To say it this way, in His death, death itself died and by His resurrection He proved that death died. Because of His resurrection, death does not rule over Him and will never conquer Him. Death cannot take the life of a man who has been raised from its bondage. Resurrection overthrows death.

Second the Bible says that when Christ died, He died to sin. Once again this echoes the truth discussed in chapter 1. Penal substitution is the center of our faith. At the heart of substitution is the reality that the One who knew no sin, was made to be sin *in our place* (2 Corinthians 5:21). When Jesus died on the cross our sin was placed on Him and he experienced the consequences of sin, which is death. He paid the penalty of our sin! Because Jesus died for our sin, He has died to sin. This means that sin and death no longer has absolute power.

Third, His resurrection made Him alive to God. His resurrection from the dead literally "made Him alive." Jesus actually died. His heart stopped pumping. He stopped breathing. The neurons in His brain stopped firing. But the good news is that He is currently raised from the dead—He lives!

When I was in middle school, the WWJD bracelets were all the rage. The colorful bands asking the question "What would Jesus do" were wrapped around the wrists of teenagers. The question was simple: if Jesus lived on earth today what would He do? But I believe the question we should be asking is this: "What is Jesus doing now?" You see Jesus isn't dead—He is alive and doing just fine (excuse my East

Texas flare). He exists as the reigning and exalted Lord. This reality shapes us personally. For us, we have to make this decision to actually belief that Jesus died and rose from the dead. If we believe this truth, its fundamentality alters our entire existence.

The Application of Our Cruciform Identity

Finally, in Romans 6:11-14 the Apostle states 3 ways we should apply this truth to our lives. In light of the fact that we are in union with Christ, we have died to our former life, and since Jesus is raised from the dead, we should *consider ourselves died to sin and alive to God.* This doesn't mean that if we think hard enough that we are dead to sin it becomes a reality. This is the cultural gospel of the power of positive thinking, which is simply tricking the mind in order to change our identity. Also, this doesn't mean that if we speak it into existence then it will become a reality. The simple truth is only God has the power to speak things into existence. By the way there is not Biblical support to suggest that we can speak our reality into existence.

Please understand that reality is not what you say you are or think you are. Reality is what God says you are in Christ as revealed in His Word. As we embrace the truth of Scripture, this transforms the way we view our new reality in Christ. In Christ sin no longer has power over us. Because of our union with Christ, He has altered our reality. By the way this change of reality and identity has already happened. So practically what we are called to do is preach the gospel to ourselves. As we struggle with sin in our lives, we can boldly declare that we have died to its power!

Following the exhortation that we have died and raised to new life, *we should not let sin reign in us.* Let's be honest. The reason we sin is because we fail to be and act as we truly are in Christ. It is not because we are spiritually bi-polar, having the Spirit and the flesh war within us. The reason is because we really don't embrace the truth of who we are in Christ. We fail to consider that truth of what God says about us in

Christ. We misunderstand our new identity in Jesus. Since we are died to sin (identity) we are called to not let sin reign in us (practice sin).

Believer you do not have to let sin rule in you. The reason why is because sin does not rule over you. You have died to your sin in Christ and now you don't have to let sin reign in you. This means that you don't have to obey sin because we have been delivered from sin. You have a new Lord and His name is Jesus not sin!

The last way we apply this truth is that now in *Christ we can offer ourselves completely to God.* Since we are already alive from the dead in Christ (spiritually), we can offer ourselves entirely to God. The Bible says that you can offer "all the parts of yourselves" to God. This is your entire being! Practically this includes your mind, heart, soul, body, finances, work, family, church, school, sex, singleness, cancer, sickness, suffering, pleasure, pain, joy, kids, house, church, and simply put everything else. God is calling every one of us to present our entire being to Him.

Putting Cruciform Identity into Practice

All of this may seem like a bunch of theological stuff that has no impact in the real world. But let's attempt to put this into practice, shall we? Let's say you are struggling with consuming porn. You're a Christian and you know that porn is harmful in many ways. But you just don't know how to overcome that particular sin. What we have discussed in this chapter provides us a paradigm for personal crucifixion.

First it is an issue of identity not primarily action. Porn is an idol and must be treated as such. The individual engaging in porn is trapped in a pattern of sin because they have been conformed into the image of their idol. Therefore, he must consider himself dead and alive. The power comes through the realization of personal identity with Christ. The old person has died and a new person has been raised.

Second since that identity in Christ is established, He treats us with grace not wrath. This encourages one to take action against the idols. The imperative is "don't let sin reign." Once the individual has acknowledged their identity with Christ, they can actively seek and destroy that sin by the Spirit. This is first of all accomplished through the Word. This destruction of our identity idols can be a slow process as the Spirit actively applies the Word to hearts.

Third the process of dying to sin isn't complete until there is an active surrender to God. You can identity your sin but you must also submit to God. This is a declaration of freedom over the besetting sin. As you exist in your identity with Christ and the Spirit works of the Word in your heart, you can freely surrender that idol to the Father. This free surrender to the Father happens through confession. The Bible promises that God is faithful and righteous to forgive sin when we confess (1 John 1:5-10).

This is our dying and rising with Jesus which creates our cruciform identity. We are in Christ because of God's grace.

So, the exhortation is to actually live out this new identity in Christ by realizing that the power of sin has been overthrown and Jesus is now our Lord. This means that in our cruciform identity we can actively seek to crucify our sin. As the power of the Spirit work in our lives, revealing our individual sin, we can "put to death" those things that seek to destroy us. This affords us the opportunity to fully surrender our lives to God through Christ in the power of the Spirit...

CHAPTER EIGHT

Experiencing Our Cruciform Identity

In *Introducing Paul*, Michael Bird writes, "Be what we are, be what we are becoming, and be what we will be on the final day of Christ Jesus."[111] Our identity in Christ is not about becoming a better person or attempting to clean ourselves up. By the way, we could never do that even if we wanted. Rather it is about being the person we already are in Christ at this moment. What this means is that as a Christian our spiritual formation is grounded in Christ. Our experience is defined by Christ, His Kingdom, and what He says in the Word. Since this is the case much of our Christian lives are dedicated to crucifying our identity idols and embracing who we are in Christ. But how do we begin to experience this cruciform identity for our spiritual formation?

Confused Holiness

Growing up I heard that I needed to do all that I could to be like Jesus. While this may be true to a certain extent, if taken to the extreme, this can result in legalism. So, I confess: I am a recovering legalist. When I became a Christian at the age of 17, I was immediately introduced to the world

---

[111] Michael Bird, *Introducing Paul: The Man, His Mission, and His Message* (Dower Groves: InterVaristy Press, 2008), pg. 136.

of legalistic holiness. My desire for growing in holiness was grounded in my own ability to manufacture that holiness by what I did and didn't do. I set up rules and regulations that dictated my life.

As I stripped away my "worldly desires," I began to realize that I wasn't growing spiritually. I went to many extremes to rid myself of the world; the typical burning of CDs, throwing out worldly movies, and getting rid of anything that would be deemed as the "appearance of evil", or so I thought. But I was still empty of joy.

I was confused about holiness. My desire to be holy—as holy as that desire may have been—was rooted in my own ability to fulfill that desire and not to rest in Christ. But as you look through the pages of the New Testament, you begin to see this remarkable theme: be who you are in Christ. This truth radically changed the way I viewed discipleship and spiritual formation. While we must work out our salvation, we must ground ourselves in the truth that it is God who works in us (Philippians 2:13).

The Gospel Narrative

In 2 Corinthians 5:17, the Bible says, "Therefore, if anyone is *in Christ*, he is a new creation. The old has passed away; and see, the new has come!" Being in Christ results in being a new creation. This marvelous truth of existing as a new creation is conditioned upon being in Christ. Here is where the nuance of "in Christ" is important. Let's unpack what it means to participate in the gospel narrative of Christ.

In Christ you have died. Galatians 2:20

The moment you trusted in Christ, something happened to you—you died to your old self. This is referring to your positional state in the eyes of God. In the eyes of God, you have already died to your sin. Yet, this truth also carries progressive implications. The process of conformity to Christ is just that—a process. It does not happen instantaneously at conversion. Rather, it is a progression of becoming what we already are in Christ, a new creation. This conformity—or in the words of Dr. Michael Gorman, cruciformity—is the way a Christian is shaped by the cross. Gorman writes, "the narrative of the crucified and exalted Christ in the normative life-narrative within which the community's own life-narrative takes place and by which it is shaped."[112]

As we surrender our hearts, minds, and wills to the cross, we participate in the gospel narrative. The union we have with Christ allows us not only to be redeemed at the moment of conversion, but it motivates us to live a life of cruciformity until we are finally united with Christ. As we discussed in chapter 6, our dying to our sin and ourselves, allows us to live freely as the cross of Christ shapes our lives.

In Christ you are raised. Colossians 3:1

We as believers share in the resurrection of Jesus already. Although we will be raised physically from the dead in the end, we now share in the benefits of the resurrection spiritually. The power of the resurrection of Jesus has present affects. Since the moment that Christ was raised from the dead, the ripple effects of the resurrection continue to make waves in the world. We were once dead in our sins but now we are raised to new life through the power of the resurrection of Jesus. This resurrection power allows us to participate in the new creation right now.

In Christ you are seated in Heaven. Ephesians 2:6

In Christ we are currently seated with him in the heavenly places. This realized view of our current position, our living in Christ now, as we will live in Christ forever, is mind-blowing. At this present time, we are already in a place of honor and prestige because of the saving act of Jesus. We are truly children of the one true King.

In Christ you will appear with Him. Colossians 3:4

---

[112] Michael Gorman, *Cruciformity*. 44.

We will share in the glory of His appearing. When Christ is publicly manifested for all the nations to see, those who are in him will also participate in His return. This act of vindication for the saints echoes many Old Testament passages, and the person that we are in Christ will one day experience that. As we trust in Christ, we enter into a new existence. We experience a change of status and identity. We are brand new people by dying and rising with Christ spiritually.

My wife and I love the TV show *Fixer Upper*. Chip and Joanna Gaines take an old house, fix it up, and make it look beautiful. They take something that was broken, ugly, and nasty turning it into something amazing. For many Christians, they view themselves as fixer uppers. But the Biblical truth is that in Christ, you can't fix yourself up. Rather, in Christ, you are brand new. You're not an old creation fixing yourself up into something new. You are a completely new person in the eyes of God—a New Creation.

Being in Christ means we are united to Him, we participate in His Risen life, we are incorporated in His death and resurrection, and we identity with Him in His exalted reign. This narrative of death, resurrection, ascension, and return is not only the gospel story about Jesus, but the story of the believer in Jesus. We are incorporated into the very life of Christ and the presence Christ is dwelling in us through the Spirit. The gospel is good news because we get to participate in it now in Christ.

Crucified Ethics

We've spent the majority of this book discussing our union with Christ as it relates to our cruciform identity. This identity finds meaning in the radical proclamation of the Crucified Christ. The cross is the basis for our identity. The Spirit empowers us to live in accordance with this new identity. The resurrection and New Creation directs our identity. The sovereignty of God undergirds our identity and God Himself secures our identity. Furthermore, our union with Christ gives us the power to overcome the power and presence of sin. It is here that we begin to transition to our spiritual formation and growth. We live in light of the Crucified One who grants us a cruciform identity. The New Testament presents for us a pattern of crucified ethics.

The Cross-Shaped Paradigm

The cross therefore shapes our morality and virtues. Jesus' death on the cross, as an act of sacrificial love and selfless obedience is the paradigm by which we live.[113]

Paul sets forth this cross-shaped paradigm in his letters. In Philippians 2:1-11, we see how the self-emptying and self-giving of Jesus provides the model for our humility. As Jesus humbled Himself, we too are to consider others more important than ourselves in humility (Philippians 2:3-4). The narrative of Jesus' experience is something that we imitate. Furthermore, in the Christ Hymn of Philippians 2, Jesus' faithfulness in obedience unto death animates our own faithfulness.[114] As we participate in the narrative of Christ through self-emptying, this results in sacrificial self-giving in love.

Additionally, in 2 Corinthians, we catch a glimpse into Paul's view of Christian ministry. The life of Jesus is manifested in our suffering (2 Corinthians 1:3-11). His life is an open display of truth that renouncing any rights of privilege (2 Corinthians 4:2). Paul is willing to embrace death in order that life may be produced in others (2 Corinthians 4:12). Additionally, the Apostle lives by the principle of power in weakness (2 Corinthians 12:9).

Consider the fruit of the Spirit: love, joy, peace, patience, kindness, goodness, faithfulness, gentleness, and self-control (Galatians 5:22). The Spirit produces these

---

[113] Richard Hays, *The Moral Vision of the New Testament: A Contemporary Introduction to New Testament Ethics* (New York: HarperCollins, 1996), 27.

[114] Hays, *The Moral Vision of the New Testament*, 32.

ethical virtues in our lives. Since we belong to Christ, our former self is crucified. So now we can live by the Spirit. Furthermore, think about the holy trinity of Christian virtue: faith, hope, and love. The Spirit also brings these about. Because we are crucified with Christ, the Spirit manifests the life of Christ in us (Galatians 2:20-21).

The transformation of our lives in Christ through the power of the Spirit is demonstrated in our practice of love.[115] Our cruciform faith is expressed in cruciform love.[116] When we serve, this is an expression of love. When you forgive, this is a demonstration of love. When you suffer on behalf of others, this is a result of love. Self-emptying and sacrificial self-giving love, therefore, is the evidence of a crucified identity.

Let me suggest that death becomes the paradigm for obedience, therefore, to obey God means that our lives are given for the sake of others.[117] Our cruciform identity, grounded in the crucified message, leads to crucified ethics.

The Language of Christian Living: Indicatives and Imperatives

When Jesus said, "Apart from me you can do nothing" (John 15:5), He actually meant we can do *nothing*. This includes living faithfully. So, when we consider Christian morality it's important to understand it is the Spirit who is working in us. Our growth in Christ is not some much of a "pick yourself up by your boots straps" mentality. Rather it is an "I need help by the Spirit" reality. Every act of obedience then is the Spirit actualizing the victory of the Risen Christ within us.[118] This victory involves a willful choice on our part and the empowerment from the Spirit.

---

[115] Macaskill, *Living in Union with Christ*, 139.

[116] Gorman, *Cruciformity*, 175.

[117] Hays, *The Moral Vision of the New Testament*, 46.

[118] Macaskill, *Living in Union with Christ*, 116.

Experiencing Our Cruciform Identity

Let's put this into practice. When you read Paul's letters you notice a specific pattern. We will call it the pattern of indicatives (simple truth realties) and imperatives (gospel commands). Often times the Apostle begins with straightforward gospel realities, and then moves into gospel commands. The commands are grounded in realities. To divorce the commands from the actual realities could result in ill-founded legalism, as in my case many years ago. The imperatives can become no more than a list of dos and don'ts without understanding that in Christ, you are already granted the ability to live them out. The point: become what you already are in Christ. Once we live within the reality of our new identity in Christ, we can then begin to live out His commands.

Let me give you some practical examples of how the indicatives of the gospel empower the imperatives of the gospel. In Ephesians 4:32 the Bible says, "Be kind and compassionate to one another, forgiving one another, just as God also forgave you in Christ." The command to be kind and compassionate to one another is grounded in the truth reality of God forgiving you in Christ. We forgive because God forgave us in Christ.

Another example is Ephesians 5:1-2, "Be imitators of God...and walk in love as Christ also loved us and gave Himself for us..." The command to be imitators and walk in love is grounded is the truth reality of Christ loving us. We love, because Christ loved us. Once our identity is grounded in Christ, we can learn to live out His Gospel commands. The Bible doesn't say to "walk in love so Christ can love you". That's legalism. Rather, it says because Christ so loved you, He gives you the power to love others.

Lastly in Romans 12:1-2 Paul writes, "Therefore...in view of God's mercies I urge you to present your bodies as a living sacrifice..." The exhortation to present your bodies as a living sacrifice is grounded in God's mercies (Romans 1-11). The entirety of our lives, actions, and character finds their foundation in Christ alone. These are just a few examples that show us that our spiritual growth and our moral formation are the outflow of our union with Christ.

Abiding in the Vine: A Picture of Spiritual Growth in Christ

As believers in Christ, we have entered into the story of redemption not just by believing in the story, but through experiencing the narrative itself in our own lives. Being in Christ means allowing the gospel narrative to shape the way we think and live. We have died, we have been raised, we are currently seated with Christ, and we will appear with Him at his coming. Because we have already experienced this gospel narrative, we can then live it out in Christ.

Once again remember the words of Jesus, *"Apart from me you can do nothing."* I didn't realize the truth of this statement until a few years ago. Let me illustrate. My wife said I needed a hobby to take my mind off the day-to-day grind of being a pastor. So, I planted a garden. I've been determined to work hard, till the soil, and labor faithfully over this small Eden in my back yard. Every day I'd go out to pull weeds, water, and wait for the results. To my surprise I began to see the results of my labors in the form of cucumbers, tomatoes, and jalapeños. This reminded me of John 15:1-8. In the text Jesus says He's the vine—the source of life. We're the branches or shoots. Jesus also says repeatedly, "Remain in me." The point is clear: as we remain in Jesus, we'll experience growth.

Jesus is the true vine, meaning He's the healthy vine. Spiritual growth begins as we remain in Him. We experience fruit, growth, and overwhelming grace as we live in Jesus. This union with Christ is the key to discipleship. Furthermore, Jesus promises if we abide in Him, we'll experience this personal growth in discipleship. At no point will the vine rot, wither, or die. This abiding in Christ is simply union with Christ.

As I worked my actual garden, I realize the importance of pruning. Pruning is different than simply ripping out the dead stuff. Pruning involves care, caution, and correction to remove the bad shoots so that the good shoots can grow. I had to remove a cucumber vine that was growing rapidly. I noticed it wasn't producing anything and was hindering the other vines. So, through careful pruning, I got rid of it. As we abide in Christ, the Father lovingly prunes us so we can grow. He corrects our direction, leads us to repentance, and graciously cleanses us from sin. The truth of the matter is God wants us to grow and flourish. And the only way to achieve that result is through the careful pruning of the Father.

As we continue to story, Jesus makes two direct statements about His Word. First, He says we're already clean because of the Word, and second, if the Word remains in us, we can ask the Father anything. The living water of the Word flows through the vine of Christ to us, the shoots. This Word produces the fruit that grow in us. As we abide in the Vine, His Word abides in us. But this Word in us is coupled with prayer. As the Word works within, prayer works it out. These two crucial spiritual disciplines are the bedrock of personal discipleship. As we soak in the Word, it saturates our lives. And prayer is how the living water of the Word works it all out in our lives. As we prayerfully read the Word, Jesus is then able to grow us, resulting in fruitfulness.

Every morning, Sophia my daughter and I walk through the garden. We see the fruit and vegetables growing after much labor. There's a sense of joy as we identity the ripe results, to the extent that my daughter's face lights up as she picks them. In a small way, I think this gives a picture of what Jesus means when He claims, "My Father is glorified by this: that you produce must fruit."

As we live in the vine, soak in water activated through prayer in the Spirit, and experience the loving pruning process, the Father is glorified in the fruit springing forth from His children. It gives the Father pleasure to see His little shoots grow and produce fruit. Jesus is laboring, cultivating, and keeping us as the New Adam. He wants His garden to grow faithfully—He wants you to grow! As I reflect on this story, here are some practical ways to apply this teaching of Jesus.

First: Abide in Christ. We must abide in Christ. Your union with Christ is the source of everything in your life. But an equally important truth must be stated as well. You're not the vine. You're not the fruit-producer; only Jesus is. We must always point people to Christ, the true vine, calling His shoots to abide in Him.

Second: Repent of Revealed Sin. As the Father loving prunes you, be quick to repent, knowing it's part of the discipleship process. As the Father reveals the wild branches, yield to the Spirit. Let Him do His work. The Father is a gracious gardener.

Third: Soak in the Word Daily. Soaking in the word is activated by prayer. If you want to grow more in love with Christ, live in His Word and pray that it takes root in your heart. We must carefully guard personal time with the Lord. We must walk with Him, hear His voice, and talk with Him in prayer.

Fourth: Bear Fruit for the Glory of God. Realize God is glorified when you produce the fruit of the Spirit. This fruit is the intended result of the Father. He desires for you and me to abide in His Son because He wants to grow us. He wants our lives to be fruitful.

This small story from Jesus paints a picture of our spiritual formation. Truth be told, spiritual growth isn't very complicated. It's a simple process. But we throw off the process if we try to cultivate the garden of our lives. We'll only grow frustrated as we try to circumvent the growing process, make our own decisions apart from the Word, and attempt to produce the fruit on our own.

This is what Jesus means when He says, "You can do nothing without me." Our spiritual formation and growth are a result of union. Our crucified identity shapes our spiritual formation.

Participating in the Gospel

When you think of spiritual formation, you may be thinking about the "spiritual disciplines" such as prayer, fasting, and reading Scripture. No doubt, these disciplines are important to the growing Christian and they should be practiced. However, the beginning of our spiritual formation is not rooted in our spiritual actions. Paul recounts in his testimony, *"I consider everything to be a loss in view of the surpassing value of knowing Christ Jesus my Lord"* (Phil 3:8). Without the Gospel we have nothing! John Calvin states:

> *Without the gospel everything is useless and vain; without the gospel we are not Christians; without the gospel all riches is poverty, all wisdom folly before God; strength is weakness, and all the justice of man is under the condemnation of God. But by the knowledge of the gospel we are made children of God, brothers of Jesus Christ, fellow townsmen with the saints, citizens of the Kingdom of Heaven, heirs of God with Jesus Christ, by whom the poor are made rich, the weak strong, the fools wise, the sinner justified, the desolate comforted, the doubting sure, and slaves free. It is the power of God for the salvation of all those who believe* ...[119]

Spiritual formation begins with knowing Christ and participating in the gospel narrative. The story of the Bible is the story we share. We are invited into God's story. It is an ongoing narrative that we don't get to make up; we simply enter in. We have entered into the grand redemptive drama of *"God reconciling the world to Himself in Christ"* (2 Cor 5:19). It is the cosmic plan of God to unite all things in Christ, things in heaven and on earth (Eph 1:10). And we are part of that story.

---

[119] https://www.thegospelcoalition.org/blogs/justin-taylor/john-calvin-at-his-gospel-saturated-best/

Understanding our spiritual formation "in Christ," as participating in the narrative drama as God unites all things together, makes holiness simply the natural outflow of knowing Jesus. Holiness is the overflow of being in Christ, because Christ is holy, not because we are holy. The disciplines are not a means to the end nor are they the end themselves. The disciplines flow from our positional standing in Christ, who is the beginning, middle, and end. We pray, we fast, and we read because we are becoming what we already are in Christ. New creational people live as new creations.

Spiritual formation is like watering a plant. You can pour water on the plant all you want, but if it isn't potted in good soil, it will not grow. We are planted in Christ. He is the vine and we are the branches. Therefore, as we receive the living water through the Word, community, and prayer, we can grow into what we already are. The reality is you are in Christ; you are free to live and think that way. Allow the gospel narrative to shape your life. May those gospel realities motivate you to live out the gospel commands. Beware of trusting in your own ability to become holy. To be holy is to be in Christ.

Be what you already are: A New Creation with a crucified identity.

CHAPTER NINE

Identity Crisis Averted

Get up...
Get dressed...
Get coffee...
Brush teeth...
Get in car...
Go to work...
Grab lunch...
Get back in car...
Come home...
Eat Dinner...
Go to sleep...
Repeat...

Sounds familiar doesn't it? The daily routine of life can be mundane and boring. The ordinary of life weighs against our soul creating within us anxiety and, in some cases, depression. There has to be something else, right? So how does a cruciform identity take that which is ordinary and turn it into the extraordinary?

It first begins by recognizing that our identity is not entirely summed up in what we do. So, for example, I am a husband, father, and pastor. Although fulfilling these responsibilities are important in my life, my identity is not defined by these important things. Don't get me wrong. I take these responsibilities seriously. However, I can only redemptively contribute in a gospel way if my identity is cross-shaped. Everything flows from who I am in Jesus. But again, what does this look like on a daily basis? How does my crucified identity in Jesus impact the daily grind of life? I want to describe this new identity in four categories.

Individually

Jesus taught that the kingdom (God's saving rule) has already arrived. Through His word and deeds, the kingdom has launched on earth though it is not fully consummated. As a result, we are living "in between the times." Our new identity is summed in this one fact: we are living as though the future has already invaded the present.[120] God's heavenly reign has come on earth. The Spirit has come, the resurrection has launched God's mission, and the Kingdom has arrived. This new kingdom reality directs the way we function here and now. This means being in Christ is grounded in this "already but not yet" kingdom truth. How does this change the way we live now?

First, it shapes our relationship with God. We don't have to wonder if we are "right" with Him, because through the death and resurrection of the Son, we are justified. This means we are set right with God on the basis of Christ's work. The barrier of sin has been broken, and now we can love God. We don't have to earn God's favor since Jesus earned it for us on the cross.

Second, since God's saving kingdom has arrived through Jesus, we can love our neighbors the way we were intended. Our love for neighbor is a telling sign regarding our love for God (see 1 John). This means my love for my neighbor demonstrates my love of God. As I serve and care of those around me, I'm doing the same thing God does for

---

[120] For more on the "already but not yet" paradigm of the Kingdom see George Eldon Ladd, The Presence of the Future: The Eschatology of Biblical Realism (Downer Groves: Eerdmans, 1996).

me. I don't have to worry about their opinions of me since my love for God is driving me to serve them. I'm not responsible for how they respond to me; I'm only responsible for loving them faithfully.

Third, the kingdom of God impacts our personal ethics. Jesus shows this in the Kingdom Manifesto, the Sermon on the Mount (Matthew 5-7). In Christ, we can do the things that seem entirely impossible, such as love our enemies, bless those who harm us, forgive those who wrong us, and fight personal sin.

Fourth, living in Christ provides us a way to commune with God through the means of spiritual disciplines. As such, Scripture communicates to us the living presence of Christ. As we soak in the Bible, we experience Christ through the Spirit and Word. His promises became ours in Christ. His truth is received in Christ. In prayer, we commune with God by sharing our needs and desires. As we fast, we hunger for God, longing to experience more of His presence. As we meditate on the glories of God, we behold Him for who He is.[121] Living in Christ, we embrace this new kingdom reality individually. We experience the resurrection power of the Spirit, which provides us all we need to know and love God.

Family

Humanity is made for community, which is first of all expressed in the family. As husbands and wives love each other according to God's design, they are ultimately pointing beyond themselves to the gospel of Christ (Ephesians 5:22-6:4). In Christ, a wife can lovingly submit to the leadership of her husband and in turn the husband can love His wife as Christ loved the church. This complementary relationship flows down to their children. The family unit is the

---

[121] See John Jefferson Davis, *Meditation and Communion with God: Contemplating Scripture in an Age of Distraction* (Downer Grove: InterVaristy Press, 2012).

basic building block of society but the unit can only function properly if Christ is the head. So practically what does this mean?

- Husbands are called to love their wives in such a way that reflects Christ's relationship to His church. A husband is called to be gentle and wise in leadership, not abusive. The husband is encouraged to be the provider, protector, prophet, and priest of his family.
- Wives are exhorted to lovingly submit to their husbands as they lead. She responds to his leadership not in begrudging submission but willingly. This doesn't mean the husband is a dictator, but rather a shepherd lovingly serving and cultivating his wife through the Word.
- The couple works together to create a home centered on Christ and His Word.
- The home becomes a place of love and hospitality.
- As parents, they are called to shepherd the hearts of their children to Christ by example and instruction.
- The family is a micro-reflection of God's macro-plan for the entire world.

Church

As already stated, the New Testament presents the truth that God's reign has arrived through the person and work of Jesus. This results in the formation of a new community (Ephesians 2:1-23). The future has irrupted in the present. The Kingdom has already arrived and the Church is the means through which the reality of God's Kingdom is manifested on earth. We are the community of the future, a signpost to the New Creation in the midst of the Old. We are an earthly reflection of the heavenly assembly.

God is actively working in the world right now to restore it and the evidence of this is the Church. We were once individuals, dead in our sin, but now we are alive in Christ. Thus, those in Christ are a New Creation (2 Corinthians 5:17-21). With this understanding, the Church is a community of hope, longing for the Day of Resurrection and renewal. We are an already/not yet people.

Living within this already/not yet paradigm shapes the way we ought to think about how the New Community functions in this world. The New Testament presents the Church as a priestly exilic community that stands in contrast to the way of the world (1 Peter 2:9-10). To say it a different way—the Church is an alternative society. This means the community of Jesus mediates God's love, grace, and mercy to a lost and broken world. As we have received love from Him, we give that love to others. This stands in contrast to a world that worships the idol of self and partakes in the sacrament of pride. The community of the Crucified and Risen One embodies His message of love to the world.

As the church hears the Word, celebrates the Lord's Supper and Baptism, and speaks the gospel, we embrace the correct view of reality. The world is living in chaos and the church provides clarity to how humanity is to function by loving, serving, forgiving, and sharing.

Community

As the church gathers together, we subsequently scatter into the world. Transformational community impact is the mission of God's people. This is seen in the way Christian's function in the workplace, marketplace, and any other place. So how can we contribute redemptively to our communities? Here are a few examples:

- Remember that Jesus is Lord and rules over every sphere of life (Philippians 2:11)

- As followers of Jesus we are ultimately citizens in exile awaiting a Better Country (Hebrews 11:16/1 Peter 1:1-2).
- We can freely proclaim Jesus to our neighbors with love (Colossians 1:28)
- Work to support your family and contribute to your community (2 Thessalonians 3:10-12).
- As followers, we should pray for our nation and its leaders as we live quiet and peaceful lives (1 Timothy 2:1-3).
- Treat each other fairly in business (Leviticus 19:11).
- As exiles we should seek the welfare of the city in which we live (Jeremiah 29:7).
- We can vote for leaders who demonstrate upright character (Proverbs 16:12).
- We can hold our leaders accountable when they demonstrate ungodly character (Proverbs 29:4).
- We can pursue peacemaking and not violence (Matthew 5:9).
- We can advocate for the God-given rights of all people (Genesis 1:26-28).
- We should prophetically call the nation to repent of wickedness (Jeremiah 18:8).
- We should take care of the oppressed (Isaiah 1:17).
- We can serve widows and orphans (James 1:27).
- Take care of the "least of these" in society (Matthew 25:31-46)

We do all of this as gospel people who have been shaped by Jesus. As we strive to live according to our identity in Christ, experiencing the reality of the Spirit and the Kingdom, we show the transcendent reality of God.

Why does living in Christ matter? It's the only way one can become fully human. This is the fullness of our cruciform identity. In Christ, we experience a new likeness as in the Garden (Ephesians 4:17-24). We often say when we fail, "I am only human." Actually, when we sin, we are demonstrating that we are less than human—we are living in a way that contradicts God's original design for our lives (Romans 1:18-32). This is why being in Christ is so important. In Him, we are actually becoming what we were intended to be in the very beginning.

Searching for the answer to the question of identity can be overwhelming. Many will say, "Just be true to yourself" while others say, "don't let anyone define you." The truth is your identity is not summed up in the criticism of others. The number of "likes" on a Facebook post does not define who you are. Your identity isn't defined by your parent's remarks at the Thanksgiving Table. It's not even created by the culture.

The liberating reality of identity is this: *In Christ, you are His*. You can now obtain the identity you long for, the one you were created to live out. As we embrace this new identity in Christ and live according to the kingdom, we can live a beautiful life by the Spirit. Everything is gradually bending towards Christ, including your life. In Christ, we know who we are, what we should do, and where we are going. In Him, we have a new identity. It is a cruciform identity.

ABOUT KHARIS PUBLISHING

KHARIS PUBLISHING is an independent, traditional publishing house with a core mission to publish impactful books, and channel proceeds into establishing mini-libraries or resource centers for orphanages in developing countries, so these kids will learn to read, dream, and grow. Every time you purchase a book from Kharis Publishing or partner as an author, you are helping give these kids an amazing opportunity to read, dream, and grow. Kharis Publishing is an imprint of Kharis Media LLC. Learn more at https://www.kharispublishing.com.